Around the World
in Twenty-Five Years

Around the World
in Twenty-Five Years

Johnny Morris

MICHAEL JOSEPH

LONDON

First published in Great Britain by Michael Joseph Ltd
44 Bedford Square, London WC1
1983

ISBN 0 7181 2229 1

Typeset by Wyvern Typesetting Ltd, Bristol.
Printed and bound in Great Britain
by Billings and Sons Ltd, Worcester.

Contents

CHAPTER ONE

Taking the Orient Express

I sometimes wonder what it would be like to be a sea anemone. To be firmly anchored to the ocean bed, just waving your arms around. Unable to move forwards, backwards or sideways. Just fixed and permanent, swaying with the lilt of the sea, having no need or desire to up anchor and travel to the four corners of the earth. To be restful.

Must be nice because the human animal is a most restless creature. Cursed with the ability of being able to put one foot in front of the other which has taken us everywhere and got us nowhere much. Well, what have we done? Run away from school, gone chasing after girls, banged our neighbour on the head, gone to war, killed people. No, to be stationary with a definite address would solve quite a few problems. But we are not. We are mobile and restless. Fortunately, some of the time we're peacefully restless, travelling the globe for the broadening of the mind and the better understanding of peoples.

And it so happened that in the late fifties Tubby Foster and I decided to take the Orient Express to Istanbul.

'Should be interesting. I mean, we needn't stay on it all the time. We can get off here and there.'

'Of course.' Tubby agreed. And we did get off here and there. We got off at Brussels, we got off at Nurenburg, we got off at Vienna and now we have just left Vienna on the way to Budapest. The railway journey from Vienna to Budapest normally takes about five or six hours but we've picked a bad day. The heavy rains have weakened the railway embankment and the line is blocked with a minor landslide. We sit in a stationary train for hours and hours.

It's a good time to check our travelling arrangements through Hungary. Remember it's in the late fifties not long after the revolution. Now, this is the situation: our visas say quite clearly in Hungarian and English that we are allowed transit only through Hungary. We mustn't stop. We must pass right through the country without getting off the train.

Now this is an extremely difficult thing to do because all trains stop at Budapest and there's often a half a day's wait before the next train leaves for Yugoslavia. Whether you are expected to sit in the railway carriage all night, or volunteer for a spot of shunting, or find a bed for the night was a matter that we had put right with the official Hungarian Tourist Agency in Vienna. They said of course you can stay the night. There is no train out until the morning, but you must book and pay for your hotel in Vienna so that everybody will know exactly where you are. We did just that.

And then quite suddenly the train jerks away. The landslide has unslid and we rattle along to the Hungarian frontier town of Heygeshalom. And at Heygeshalom a shuffling posse of slack-trousered troops search the train. It's an interesting demonstration. They tramp up the corridors, they peer around the compartments, they crawl underneath the carriages the entire length of the train. They are sullen and grim. They don't speak. They seem to hate what they're doing, themselves, each other, us, *everything*. And then they give up their treasure hunt and the train slides away, and we arrive in Budapest at 11.30 at night.

Most cities look pretty at night. Budapest is built on a cluster of hills and it twinkles and glows cosy and promising in the distance. But when we get out of the train and drag our bags outside the station we get a bit of a shock. The large forecourt is gloomy and empty. A few pale yellow lights flicker behind the trees in the street. A weary lumbering tram dragging four reluctant carriages behind it goes grinding and grizzling into the night. The station stands gaunt and old, coughing quietly in the smoke.

Well, we know the name of our hotel but how do we get there?

'Bit of a problem, isn't it?'

There are no taxis. And then a man comes over to us.

'Excuse me, you're English aren't you?'

'Yes.'

'Can you tell me what's the word for taxi in this blasted language?'

'I think it's the universal word—just taxi.'

'Thanks very much.' And he strides into the street. 'Taxi! Taxi! Taxi!'

It's a brave effort but he might as well shout for a pot of tea and a plate of tripe. We eventually ambush a taxi in the street at about half past twelve and hammer away to our hotel. Thank goodness, the receptionist speaks English.

'We've booked rooms here.'

'That's quite right.'

'Good.'

'We have the booking.'

'Good.'

'But you cannot stopping here.'

'Why not?'

'We have not the room.'

'But we booked.'

'That's quite right.'

'And you accepted.'

'That's quite right.'

'Well, then?'

'We have not the room. We have transferred you to another hotel.'

'Oh, and supposing they have not the room?'

'Hahahaha, I think so.'

'Hahahaha, I hope so.'

By a stroke of luck we find another taxi just roaming the streets outside and he takes us to our new hotel. It's a strange place. It looks as though the manager left for King Edward VII's funeral and never came back. A dead crystallised chandelier still manages to cling to the ceiling, a few cracked leather chairs crouch and wince in the corner and hope they'll never be sat on again, and from a restaurant somewhere in the back a gipsy orchestra sobs and blubbers a desperate Hungarian air. *Tararararara.*

The receptionist obviously knows we are coming but he doesn't speak any English, German or French.

'Passeport!'

Tubby Foster hands over his passport with a sweet smile. The receptionist looks at it and then with a tired contempt flings it down on the counter and says, *'Bdupertroyvaros tarararara.'* There is no possible way of finding out what he means.

'That's no way to treat a British passport. Look, I'll have a try with mine—he probably doesn't like your passport picture.'

My passport is flung down on the counter. What's the matter with him? We'll never get anywhere at this rate.

'Look, we want bed. Understand—bed, dormir, schlafen, sleep, a bit of kip, got it?'

'Buperrutroyvaros tarararara.'

'Er, can I help you?'

'Mmm, oh!'

A dark strange-looking man is standing behind us. He's wearing a trench coat and trilby. He looks just as though he's stepped out of a spy film.

'Well, there's something he doesn't like about our passports.'

'Yes I heard, your visa is for transit only. You are not allowed to stay at hotels anywhere in Hungary.'

'But the official tourist agency accepted our visas, our booking and our money.'

'It's a great pity. Just a moment, please.'

He talks to the receptionist. It's odd, but we can almost understand what the receptionist says back. It would translate roughly like this: *Buperlctorogvaros.* Look, I've nothing against these people personally. *Uchtrongglibrad.* But you know these transit visas as well as I do. *Uchtronvagarosh.* I meant, I've got my job to think of. *Uchprodmoy.* Supposing something was to happen? *Notchcoreyiava.* I'd be right up the flipping creek, mate, *notchcoreyiava*, up the creek, mate, *notchcoreyiava*, up the creek, mate.

They talk for some time and then the strange dark man

comes to us. We must be patient, we must sit down and wait for a few minutes. All right, let's sit in the restaurant. The leader of the orchestra comes wandering over and sobs his violin right over our table. *Tarararar.*

What's the name of that tune? They have stolen our horses. They have stolen our horses, *tararar.* What is the receptionist doing? He has phoned the police. *Tarararar.* They have stolen our horses, they've slept in our beds, they've told us fibs and now they've sent for the police.

We sit and sit. The orchestra whimpers its way through one sad song after another. They have just finished 'Someone Kicked Auntie when she was Hoeing Last Week'.

'Excuse me, I will see if we have some news.'

'Oh, thank you.'

'I will be back.'

'Who do you think he is?'

'Well, he's a copper.'

'Secret police?'

'Yes.'

'Look, let's have a bottle of wine and see if we can get pinched for drinking after hours. After all, it's nearly three o'clock.'

'Good idea.'

We call a waiter. 'Er, wine—you know?'

'Yes, yes.'

The waiter goes away and comes back with a bottle of Tokay and a small Union Jack. He places the Union Jack carefully in the middle of our table, pats it gently and smiles.

The secret copper comes back. 'The police have telephoned. They say you must leave on the eight o'clock train tomorrow morning.'

'But we can stay here?'

'Yes, you can stay for the night.'

'What's left of the night.' It's all very unfortunate.

'Goodnight.'

'Goodnight.' He pivots easily on a heel and glides out into the night.

And a few hours later we get a taxi to catch the eight o'clock train. Our driver is a handsome burly man—he

11

slings his taxi around with a deliberate carelessness. Mind you, he's got plenty of room to do it in. There are hardly any private cars in Budapest. Every time we sweep around the corner the driver turns round to us and grins. His teeth are made of steel. A mouth full of functional engineering. He smiles a dull, machined-steel leer. It gives him a slightly mad look. You half expect him to take a spanner out of his pocket and champ it up into little bits. I wonder if they go rusty overnight and leave brown toothprints in the morning's bread and butter . . .

And we scream across Budapest. It was once a beautiful city. It still is, but now it sits pensive and sad like a widow in an inglenook staring into the angry embers of memory.

'What time do we get to Belgrade?'

'About eight tonight.'

'Twelve hours—might be able to get a bit of a snooze in.'

And we half-doze and with tired eyes watch the great Hungarian plain slowly turn around as we lumber on.

We arrive at Kelebia, the frontier post between Hungary and Yugoslavia, at about 11.30. Passport control. Passports. The passport official is pale and ill and he has got chocks of wadding bunged in his ears. It isn't even white wadding—it's yellow wadding. He looks like a tallow candle. He just looks at our passports, closes his eyes, then opens the window and goes: 'Tembrukkoyyoi'. We didn't know at the time, but it meant 'Turn out the guard, and call Madame Kloplosh, we've got a right lot here.' Within half a minute a clumping platoon of soldiers with automatic rifles had got us surrounded and Madame Kloplosh comes creaking down the corridor. Madame Kloplosh is obviously an interpreter and interrogator. Madame Kloplosh is wearing a black leather mackintosh, her hair is mud grey and Eton cropped. She is probably about sixty but looks over eighty. Her face is like a large, dead, autumn-rhubarb leaf. She speaks a lot of Hungarian and a little German.

Our visas aren't in order. We should, she said, go out on another line, not this one. What difference does it make? No difference, but we have broken quite a lot of laws and we must get off the train for examination and interrogation. An officer says 'Prennoyskorya', which means 'Come on then, let's have yer'. We drag our suitcases from the racks. The soldiers just stand and watch us. We are marched about a hundred yards down the track to the customs house and locked up in a room. Two soldiers are posted at the door and the rest are sent to search the underneath of the train.

Well, here we are in the nick.

'What do you think they are going to do?' I ask.

'You can't tell,' says Tubby.

It's quite a comfortable nick really. It's got four easy chairs, a table, a radio in the corner and an uninterrupted view of the railway line and the flat sodden Hungarian plain. *Phweoo.* That's that. There goes our train. We scramble to the window and watch the last carriage get smaller and smaller as it gathers speed for Yugoslavia and freedom.

'You know, this isn't funny.'

'No, I know it isn't.'

'When do you think they'll let us go?'

'This year, next year, sometime, never.'

Then the door opens and in stump about eight uniformed sullen officials. There are chocolate uniforms, buff uniforms, pale green uniforms and some very sinister looking gents in assorted freelance mufti.

The head chocolate major knows four words of English. I imagine he knows these four words in every European language. He salutes and, believe it or not, says 'Which is the leader?'

Which is the leader? 'Well, we don't have a leader, we're just friends.'

'No leader?'

'No, no leader.'

This narks the chocolate major. We are stalling, being evasive, cunning.

'Which is the leader?'

'Well, I'm not going to be the leader.'

'No, nor me—they usually shoot the leader first.'

'Wohin gegen sie?'

'Istanbul.'

'Warum?'

'Why . . . er . . . holiday—vacance.'

'Wohin gegen sie?'

'Istanbul.'

'Warum?'

'Holiday.'

'Which is the leader?'

'No leader, kine leader.'

'You are the leader?'

'No, I'm only the fullback.'

'Fullback. Fullback wohin gegen sie?'

'Istanbul.'

'Warum?'

'God knows.'

'Fullback?'

'Yes.'

He wants to inspect our suitcases. The search lasted three to four hours. They search the hems of handkerchiefs, the cuffs of shirts. Dirty socks are held up to the light and turned inside out. They confiscate our Hungarian money but they give us a receipt for it.

Then another gentleman turns up. He's in a very different uniform. He's got slit, sly eyes and a bulbous nose. He's a sort of ace investigator. When all else fails then he's the boy for finding out who's telling whoppers. He's had some cringing, snivelling specimens through his hands at one time and another, and he's scared the pants of bigger blokes than us. The pant-scarer then puts on an astonishing performance. It's grotesquely comic but rather frightening. There is an empty cigarette packet lying on the table. He picks it up, his face pulls into an awful leer and then he tears the packet up with a terrible violence into tiny pieces and hurls them on to the table. It's as though he's having an epileptic convulsion. Then he advances on Tubby Foster and stares him straight in the eyes. It's all become silly and funny. Tubby starts to giggle and so do I. It drives the pant-scarer mad. He'll have another convulsion in a minute. We don't see him have it—he stamps out of the room.

The other investigators just watch us. Their faces are like plaster casts. Their eyes are dead and dull. They stare unseeing, like stuffed animals in a museum. Their intelligence seems to have been drilled away and wadding stuffed in. Perhaps that was what was coming out of that chap's ears? It is impossible to make any sort of contact with them. Can we telephone? No. Eat? No. Drink of water? No. Lavatory? No. Would they like a cigarette, then? No. And then they turn and stride away.

It's wonderful what hunger will make you do. It turns the tremulous man into an adventurous fool. The last decent meal we had was lunch in Vienna nearly two days ago. We are both very hungry now. We've been shut up for six hours and now we're left alone.

'You know, I'm hungry,' says Tubby.

'So am I. I'm going to make a scene.'

I try the door and it opens. They are going to leave us alone, perhaps. The guards make no attempt to stop us. Well, you couldn't escape from a desert like this.

We know there's a café somewhere about but we haven't any money. There's an officer leaning against the wall. I wave the receipt for the money they've confiscated. 'Ich habe nicht das gelt. Ich kunnen nicht essen, ich kunnen nicht drinken. Gaben mir das gelt, gaben mir das gelt.'

He looks straight through me and walks away.

There's another one: 'Ich habe nicht das gelt, ich kunnen nicht essen. Ich kunnen nicht drinken. Gaben mir das gelt, gaben mir das gelt.'

He shrugs and pushes me aside. Then we see old wadding-ears. 'Hey, ich habe nicht das gelt, ich kunnen nicht essen, ich kunnen nicht drinken.'

He sneers and goes off to search a goods train.

There's another: 'Hey, ich habe nicht das gelt . . .' I shall be doing this on this station in twenty years time, it seems. I'll get myself worked into a folk song. 'An old man is standing on ze railway station and wis ze passers-by he is imploring that he has no money and is very hungry. Ich habe nicht das gelt, Ich habe nicht das gelt, Ich kunnen nicht essen, Ich kunnen nicht drinken.'

Oh come on, this looks like the main office. We storm in. All our graven image friends are there posing for some more

15

sculpture. They aren't a bit surprised to see us. I do my bit another five times and finish the last chorus banging the table and yelling: *Geben mir das gelt! Geben mir das gelt!* Well, we're hungry. The chocolate major blinks once, opens a drawer and gives me the money. Danke schone, danke schone, why wouldn't you do it in the first place? We scuttle out like two naughty children, giggling.

'I say, we're asking for it, you know.' Tubby worries.

There's a café down the road, we could see it from our prison. Road? It's just a flat, wide, mud track with unornamental ponds sunk in it.

The café is a shack. Good pull-up for ox-drivers. The man at the bar is hostile.

'Bread?'

'Nein.'

'Salami?'

'Nein.'

Nothing to eat at all. Drink? He ladles some stuff out of a churn. Mmm, it's like vinegar and battery acid.

There are a few other civilians in the shack and we learn that they are the Israeli chess team travelling back to Israel. They were hauled off the train, as we were, for interrogation.

The hostile barman is leaning on the bar devouring a cigarette, suck, suck. The hairs on his chest bristle out of his shirt as a sort of warning. He gets ready to give us some more battery acid and lemon.

'No, no, no. There's a bottle on the shelf—that one, *that* one.'

He pulls the cork. It's quite a good wine. The Israeli chess team sit together in the corner. They've got a set of chessmen with them and they begin to work out chess problems. One of them speaks English, German and Hungarian and he tells us that he's heard that we are going to be put on the eleven o'clock train for Belgrade that evening. It's now eight o'clock.

The barman puts on another cigarette and he's raging like a blocked-up fireplace. Smoke erupts out of all the holes in his face. He's glaring at us in rather a frightening, desperate way. He's not all that sober either, because he accidentally drops a glass. He doesn't bother to pick it up—he steps on it. *Crrrrkkkk*. And then he paces up and down the bar glaring at us and tramping through the glass: *crrk, crrk, crrk*.

Suddenly he strides over to the door, slams it and clatters an iron bar across it. Then he bashes the shutters shut. He goes over to the Israeli chess team.

'Uchpredorsay.'

'He wants to know where you are going,' an Israeli translates.

'Istanbul.'

'Predork Istanbul. I want to go to Istanbul. Uchpredoray. I don't want to stay here, I want to go to Istanbul.'

His face has completely changed. His hostility has vanished. It was a façade, a pose—now he's smiling at us. It is a dreadful smile. Full of warmth, emotion, fear and envy.

'Uchpremoyko Istanbul. I want to go to Istanbul.'

We are not sure whether we are going to get there ourselves. He understands. Nemdroyask. You must all have a drink with me. He suddenly skips away like a little boy who's going to do some shopping for mummy. He comes back with two bottles of wine and some glasses. He drops a glass and walks on it, *crrkcrrkcrrk*. Hahaha! Uchprondervos. What's a blasted glass between friends? He dashes the wine out with a terrifying abandon. We throw it back. More, more!

Phwee. That's our train. We must finish the wine. The barman clasps us with a great bearlike affection. He unbolts the doors, we dash over to the station and scramble on to the train. It's unbelievable, we're free, they're letting us go! Goodbye, Kelebia, good riddance! We hope that one day . . .

Look! There, heavy and sad under the lamplight, is the barman. He wants to go to Istanbul. We wave to him. Goodbye. He looks quickly left and right and then, with his hand held tight to his chest, he just flickers his fingers at us. He's frightened to wave. *Ffffsss*. We flicker our fingers at him, *fffssssss*. As our train pulls away we watch him until he's a tiny yellow dot in the distance.

There are two sorts of Hungarians. There are the chiselled

officials with wadding in their ears, and there are the civilians—warmhearted, emotional, hotblooded, affection-ate. We met mostly the wrong sort.

But then it's the late fifties and everybody everywhere is just a bit jumpy and not very prosperous as yet, except Tubby Foster and myself. Well, we had stayed in Belgrade for a day or two and changed rather too much English money into Yugoslav dinars, and the bank has told us that they will not change them back. We're stuck with a wad of dinars that we have to spend.

'Now, that's not expensive is it?' It's a sort of penny whistle—the sort that the shepherds play.

'No, but I don't think I want a whistle,' Tubby says.

'Those beetroots look quite nice.'

'Yes, but what can you do with a beetroot?'

'Mmmm. There's a toy saxophone?'

'No, thanks.'

'I tell you what!'

'What?'

'Let's spend our dinars on dinners!'

'Ah, get something to eat.'

'Yes, find a posh restaurant and blow it.'

Well, let's see. That place looks expensive, quite posh. And we go in. But it's not half as posh as we thought. There's not a speck of decoration anywhere—just a picture of Marshal Tito. Sitting to the right of us is a dwarf. A lady dwarf. She's got a giant-size bottle of medicine of some sort and she's just taken her third spoonful. Obviously must be taken before meals. Perhaps it's to make her grow. On the left is a man, a very nice man, eating a sheep's head. A sheep's head on a plate with gravy. He loves sheep's head. I can hear him: *sllusssssmack*! I can't take my eyes off him. He's picked up the laughing grey head and is really going it now. Brown gravy tears run out of the empty eye sockets, and he smacks a passionate kiss on the side of the sheep's nose. *Ssssssmack*. And another, *sssmack*, and another, *sssmack*! It's the most ghoulish love scene . . .

'You know, I've longed for this moment (*baaasmack*). Oh

18

my darling (*baaasmack*). Come here! I could eat you! (*baaaasmack*) . . .'

All the diners in the restaurant are staring at us. We must look very funny to them. Yet there's a man eating a sheep's head on one side of us, and a dwarf hitting the medicine bottle on the other but *we* are the ones that get stared at.

Here's the waiter with the menu. It doesn't mean a thing. It's an entirely different language. What can we have? I'm sure whatever we choose we'll get a sheep's head. We point at the menu anywhere. It's like picking a horse with a pin. Probably *is* horse. The waiter slips away.

He comes back with two sheep's heads on plates. He's a proper little Salome. I don't think I can manage one. Oh, thank goodness, they're not for us. The dwarf gets one and the other goes to the lucky gentleman by the door. We get a kind of stew, some salad and a bottle of wine. And it's not bad at all.

And as we come out to make our way to the station the waiter is still carrying sheep's heads about.

The Orient Express is hardly an express after Belgrade. It slows down quite a bit and through Bulgaria to Istanbul it seems to scarcely get up to thirty miles an hour. But the journey through Turkey is quite fascinating. It is a most ancient country and the people are tough, durable and strong individuals.

And we eventually reach Istanbul. Istanbul is something such as we've never seen before. It's like one tremendous market. Intricate, involved, complicated; tiny alleys, narrow streets jammed full of carts, donkeys, horses, men, women, kids, trams, dirt, filth, and junk. Letter-writers, boot-blacks, people eating melons, spitting pips, and going to sleep—but it's the carriers that are the most amazing things in Istanbul. Yes, the carriers. You have to keep reminding yourself that they are human beings because they behave like pack horses.

The steep, ramshackle, honeycomb construction of Istanbul imposes a terrible transport problem. In certain parts it's quite impossible for lorries, carts or even donkeys to get about and so this incredible tribe of carriers has cropped

19

up. They are men who just carry things. But what *things*. They wear a sort of harness on their backs with a bit of a platform on it. Then they bend over at right angles and allow themselves to be loaded. They are like handicapped mules with only their two hind legs on the ground, and two forelegs that just dangle as they walk.

But look what they carry. There's one with a refrigerator on his back, there's another with a treadle sewing machine, there's one with a whole shop-front, glass and all, and there's one with a wardrobe *and* two beds, and there's one with two best-quality, brass-handled coffins. Everything is humped and carried. The carriers blunder and sweat bow-legged everywhere. It's an astonishing sight. It's like suddenly uncovering an ants' nest. See how they struggle and crawl over one another with their impossible egg burdens. There doesn't seem to be any sort of overall plan—no organisation. Everyone works for himself doing tiny little deals with someone else. There's a constant movement of job-lots of tomatoes, melons, motor tyres, carpets, old machinery—and it's all carried. The entire produce to feed a city of two million is carried.

It's a tiring place, Istanbul. You can never stand back and calmly look at the canvas. No, here the canvas is bunged right underneath your nose and every inch of it crammed with some startling scene, some hopeless activity or distressing spectacle. There is a tremor of tension in the air, a suspicion of violence, a whiff of murder, and everybody is up to something. The great oriental bazaar manages to pack in over 4,000 shops under its great roof. Steamships belch out black smoke as they bash up and down the Bosphorus.

We take a ferry across the Bosphorus to Asia Minor and look back at the city. And out here Istanbul becomes the romantic city we always imagined it to be. The mosques stand proud and beautiful, the golden domes shine in the sun, the minarets pierce the brash blue sky and the frantic huggermugger trapped in the tight stonework close to the ground is hidden.

That evening we found a little restaurant called the Pic Nic. It had fine tablecloths and on each table was a little vase with just one arum lily in it. It was old fashioned but clean and the food was very good. Now that was in the 1950s when the world was still trying to recover from the war. Last year I went back to Istanbul, and do you know it was much the same. It had hardly changed at all. A few skyscrapers had appeared, but not many. There were still quite a few carriers about, still humping wardrobes, and some steamships still hooted to and fro to Asia Minor.

And the Pic Nic restaurant? It's still there. And it's still the same, with an arum lily in a little vase on every table. It is exactly the same. It hasn't moved, it hasn't changed. And where and what have I done in the twenty odd years between my visits to the Pic Nic? Nearly worn myself out bashing about all over the place, but the Pic Nic is still there, like the sea anemone. Just like the sea anemone.

CHAPTER TWO

Venetian Bats and Vesuvian Bugs

When you choose to travel about the world instead of staying happily in one place you do make yourself quite vulnerable. The world is full of nasty little traps and great big horrible shocks. That beautiful country of Italy is full of traps, surprises and shocks. And the most memorable shock I think that Tubby Foster and I got was the day that we arrived at Venice.

'I say, that's never Venice, is it?' asked Tubby.

'Well, according to the map and the road signs that *is* Venice.'

'But it doesn't look a bit like Venice. It looks like Wolverhampton!'

Well, don't forget we are still on the mainland and there's a tremendous lot of industry around here. Venice, after all, is built on islands out at sea, but it is difficult to believe that Venice is not far away. Great concrete water coolers gasp at the sky, vigorous chimneys pump out thunder clouds of bad breath, and the whole place is scrawled over with a prickly bramble of pylons and wires. And this is just about as far as we can go.

'Where are you going to leave the car? I know you can't take a car into Venice,' said Tubby.

'Can I help you, please gentlemen?'

Oh, a policeman. There's so much we want to know, it's a job to know where to start! 'Well, you see, we are sort of travelling about and what with one thing and another it's a bit diff . . .'

'You wish to stay in Venice?'

'That's right.'

'For one night, two night, three night?'

'Oh, for two night.'

'Put your car in that garage there, and book your hotel there.'

'Oh thank you very much.'

'Please don't mention it.'

I must say it's all extremely efficient. We park the car in an enormous eight storey concrete car warren, book an hotel at the information centre and catch the water bus for St Mark's Square. It's an incredible boat ride. We push away from the pier—an ordinary little pier in an ordinary little canal. Might be anywhere on the canal around the back of Regent's Park. Then we turn a corner and get the biggest shock of our lives. Don't forget we've just emerged from behind a forest of factory chimneys, for suddenly there is Venice. The Venice that Canaletto and Guardi painted. Just as they painted it. It hasn't changed.

It's a weird sensation, to be floating through an unbelievable picture that you've known by heart since childhood. We had a picture of Venice pasted on a big screen in the bedroom when we were children. It was next to a Louis Wain cat with a bib and tucker on, eating a pot of what was labelled 'mouse cream'. A cat with a pot of mouse cream was, of course, a bit of make-believe—but so was this place Venice. A very extravagant bit of make-believe. And now we're sailing through it.

Look at the gondolas, with their battle-axe heads rearing out of the water—dozens and dozens of them swimming around like monstrous cormorants; the gondoliers in striped shirts and straw hats with ribbons on, shoving their black, quaint craft through the choppy water; the delicate marble palaces grouped side by side; the gay, striped poles rising sideways out of their quivering reflections. This is the picture on the old screen. It hasn't changed.

Oh yes it has. There's a set of traffic lights at the cross canals, shining green for us. We go over. There's a small flotilla of craft in the side canal waiting to come out. There go the lights, and here they come like ducks scrabbling for a

23

gobbet of bread. This must be the rush hour. It is.

We land at St Mark's Square and struggle along with our awkward luggage. The square is alive with the most fascinating collection of people. All just strolling around. French priests, Brazilian soldiers, Italian sailors, German nuns, Swiss monks, Corsican bandits, Sicilian spivs and a lady artist from Peebles in a tartan skirt.

There's a band standing in the square playing 'Colonel Bogey', *tatatata*. There's a rattle like someone flipping through the pages of a tremendous floppy book and the air is splattered with smacking pigeons. The sun gets freckles and splutters. *Tararara*. The pigeons glide and flutter back down again. The ground trembles with pigeons. Look: when someone throws a handful of corn they all scoot towards it like grey iron filings to a magnet. *Tarara*.

Now we've booked ourselves in at a very cheap hotel and we can't find it—that's twice we've been around the square. *Tarararar*. And eventually we find it up a little alleyway beside a tiny black canal.

'I say, can you smell anything?'

'Not half can you,' Tubby agreed.

'Mmm, yeah, what is it do you think?'

'It's that canal.'

I'm afraid it is. I so hoped that it wasn't. Well, it's one of the popular ways of dismissing Venice. It is now and it was twenty-odd years ago. 'Venice? My dear, the pong, *phew*.' Well, there is a pong. It's a pong that you can't forget. It hangs in the nostrils of the memory, but I will say this for it—it moves around and so you don't get obsessed by it. Sometimes our little canal was pretty middling and at other times, well, he was as sweet as a nut. It's a matter of luck.

You see, Venice was built in this strange location mainly for defence reasons. In the fifth century the people living on the mainland in the coastal areas were constantly attacked by barbarians from the mountains, and so they moved out to this collection of small islands because it was safer. There are about 120 islands cluttered tightly together like a handful of broken biscuits thrown in a puddle, and on these islands Venice grew rich and lovely. Hundreds of little bridges clipped the islands together and for centuries the garbage has flowed into the sea. Now there's not much tidal movement in Venice and although the main Grand Canal is flushed out fairly thoroughly every day, the little canals that curl around the back sometimes lie doggo for days and there you get a pong.

It's not all that bad really, but it's the more noticeable when you happen to be gazing at the beautiful tower of a church and *phew* there it is, or leaning on a tiny bridge watching a gondola drift by in the evening, the gondolier gently easing it along because he's taking two lovers for a romantic dreamglide around the islands. You can almost hear the music, *trararrbarcarolltararara*, the most perfect setting in the world for love's young/middle-aged/old dream . . .

The girl has dreamt about this for years and at last this is it. Pity about those two men leering from the bridge though. She hadn't thought of an audience. There are people watching all over the place. Poor girl, she imagined that just about by the bridge here she and Allister would go into a mad gulping embrace. Not a hope. This tunnel of love has no proper tunnel. And it's very difficult to sit in a gondola and look natural. There's a terrible temptation to start acting—well, you've seen so many film stars floating around in gondolas acting out the perfect romantic night, but they've always had a script to work to.

'Brenda darling, you do realise, don't you, that the wise old men of the past built Venice entirely for you?'

'Hahaha! Allister, you're being ridiculous.'

'I feel ridiculous/inadequate/helpless when I'm beside you, Brenda.'

'Allister, you're such a child, hahaha!'

Allister: '*Grrrrrr.*'

Tararar. That's how it should go, but it doesn't. Well, Allister's sitting there bolt upright. He's not going to start any messing about in full view. Brenda goes straight into page four of her script: 'Allister, look at those little statues up there. Aren't they lovely, hahahah,'—sniff—*phew*, she's suddenly got the pong. I see her nostrils bulge and fall and she darts a glance at Allister. *Phew*, Allister's got it too and starts looking around the gondola to see what it is. Bravely Brenda ploughs on with page four. 'Aren't those window boxes simply heavenly, hahaha?' Here she should just trail a hand in the water. She nearly does but just stops in time. Had she done so she would have shaken hands with the yellow claw of a chicken, and even if she'd missed that, close behind the claw there is a large unidentified floating object. She gazes at it with horror as it limps by. I think she's identified—*tararararara*! And they sail stiffly, awkwardly away, *tararararara*.

No, it's a job to get romantic about the canals, they are such fascinating collectors of evidence. And as all we criminals know, it's very difficult to get rid of the evidence. Now there's a whole drama behind that bit of evidence. A dead pigeon drifting along. A yard behind him a dead cat. Just missed him. They obviously got locked in mortal combat on the top of a tower somewhere, missed their footing and toppled in. And watching them both from the green slime steps of a warehouse is a cynical, thoughtful brown rat nibbling a decaying corn on the cob. I think he pushed them.

It doesn't seem fair on Venice that these sordid little pictures should push their way in line with the radiant gold-blue brilliance of St Mark's Cathedral, the delicate filigree beauty of the Doge's palace. Still, they do, and you've got a job to avoid them and you can't forget them.

You can't forget the evening promenades in Venice either. The evening lights glowing, the band playing in the square (*trararara*), every nationality in the world strolling around the beautiful square. It's then that the bats come out on the prowl. Human bats. Yes, great big human bats. Dracula's cousins, dozens of them. In black smoked glasses and sleek oiled hair, their black wings folded back underneath their gaberdine casings they come slinking around to see what's about. They are looking for girls. Not in a gay amorous way but in a sinister, menacing manner. They're after blood. I think they try some form of hypnosis to begin with because they pick out a victim and stare and stare and stare at it at almost point blank range.

Look at that middle-aged bat. He's picked out a nice-looking English girl, a real Penelope, sitting at a café table with her mummy and daddy. The bat is fluttering a few feet from their table eyeing Penelope all over, blowing smoke out of his nose, his black eyes following the line of her white neck and her shoulders down under the table, slipping over her healthy hockey legs and then back up again. Daddy is getting perturbed. What's this fellow want? Mummy is all of a do-dah. Don't you think we ought to be going? Penelope, a pale pink, looks down her drinking straw into her orangeade and quite forgetting herself blows a clutch of bubbles *bubblebubblebubble*. If Mummy and Daddy were to leave Penelope for a second you feel the bat would swoop in and sink his fangs in her neck.

The younger bats are perhaps worse. They hunt in twos, threes and small packs. They circle the victim and begin a shrill bat-whistle, *whew whew*, then they form into a line, fly in and block her way. Only by swinging her handbag and catching the leader a fourpenny one can the victim get away. The bats don't like that. They skedaddle off into the night.

A few days later we drive across Italy towards Naples. We curve through beautiful mountains, slide around pale yellow rivers and arrive at Naples.

'Hey, here, you wanta watch? I just gotta the one left.'

'No thank you, go away.'

'Why you saya go away? You no see me watch.'

'No thank you, go away.' He goes away but to speak harshly does come a little unnaturally to the diffident English.

'You likea nicea jewellery, very good?'

'No thanks.'

'You take this for the woman 5,000 lire?'

'No.'

'Justa 5,000 lire.'

'No, go away.'

Oh dear. There are too many people in Naples. There're thousands and thousands of them. Look up that steep old alleyway there. The washing is hanging as thick and heavy

27

as the foliage of a tropical forest. There must be fifty thousand old sheets, shirts, skirts, pants and goodness knows what else swinging up there, thankful for a breath of fresh air. Down below the alley is alive with people. Just like a bit of an anthill, all scratching, struggling away at something or other in the alley. Some cobbling, some stitching, some tinkering, some running, some hobbling, some coughing, some spitting, some sleeping, some crying, some dying. Look: there's a man trying to sell a disappointed-looking octopus, another with a wriggling bucket of eels, another with a dead hare and one with a big tin bath stacked with black and dangerous mussels.

And look where the ants live, in dingy squalid little stables. Tubby Foster thinks it would make a good photograph. Immediately he takes his camera out of its case a large Italian lady comes waddling over.

Careful, we've got to be careful here. You know people get touchy when you pry into their lives. She points to the camera.

'Photographi?'

'Yes, si, photographi. Is that all right?'

'Oh bella, bella.' She turns and looks at her beloved alleyway—at the washing and the squalor. She stretches out her arms in ecstasy. Oh bella, bella! There's no better picture to be had in the whole of Italy. She calls her friends. Of course, no place like it in the world. Can they be in the picture, smiling like this—*hahahahah*? Oh yes, the Neapolitans are warmhearted, generous people. By our standards many of them live in dreadful poverty but they're happy and if you're happy then you're not really poor.

We wander down by the waterfront where the little cafés and restaurants cluster together. It's in these cafés, the guide book tells us, that you can hear genuine Neapolitan songs sung to the accompaniment of guitars and mandolins. Well, we'd quite like a bit of that. We go in.

The menu is one of the most fascinating we've seen for a long time. It's written in English. Steak in the manner of Bismark, steak in the manner of the hunter. Tail of toads. They mean toad of holes, toad in the hole? No, tail of toads.

Mmmm, need a lot of tail for a mouthful. Fish to grill and ice cream into the cup. I like that—ice cream into the cup. In England we have ice cream into the wafer and chips into the paper . . . We play safe and try steak in the manner of the hunter. He must have been a pretty rotten shot. Still, the gravy's good.

And here come the Neapolitan songsters. Three of them, one guitar, one mandolin and one with a dirty piece of paper in his hand. Now what's that for? They're a shifty-looking trio. I'm sure I saw that one selling fountain pens this morning. They start. *Tararara, Videomarequantobello spirt tantosentimente*. The singer sings without opening his mouth and he reads his words from his dirty scrap of paper. He can hardly sing and they can hardly play. *Turna a soriento fame compa*. And that concludes the entertainment for today. One song and they're around with the collection plate and we cough up.

We're always coughing up. There was the time when we were stopped at a level crossing. The pole is across the road, there's a train due. Suddenly there's a chap cleaning our windscreen. It doesn't need cleaning.

'Did you order this bloke to clean the windscreen?' Tubby asked.

'You know I didn't. Where did he come from?'

'I don't know.'

'I mean, we are way out in the country.'

It takes him five seconds to take about five swipes at the windscreen and then there's a great paw in through the window clawing for money. All right, we give him some. He's not very pleased about it but the funny thing is this: we were so taken aback by the whole business that we didn't notice a train go through, because suddenly the bar lifts and over we go.

'Well, what do you make of that?' I ask.

'Smart boys, aren't they?' replies Tubby.

It certainly looks as though the windscreen washer and the signalman are in the fiddle together. One stops the cars—there don't have to be any trains about—and the other washes the windscreens and they split the lire. It's a simple form of banditry.

And so you get terribly suspicious after a bit. Like the time we drove out from Naples to take a look at Vesuvius. Vesuvius is not very far from Naples. It doesn't take long to get there and it shouldn't take long to get to the top as there's a chair lift to take you right to the crater. Only we can't seem to find it. We've followed the notices too—Vesuvius straight on, Vesuvius turn right; Vesuvius—hello, what's this? A little ticket office on the side of the road. This where we pay, I suppose. We stop. A man comes slinking out. A very familiar type. Smooth black hair, brown flat face and black glasses. It's impossible to see where he's looking or if he's got eyes at all, they just look like sightless holes. And yet he peers into the car.

'You English eh?'

'Yes. All right for two?'

'Yes, for two.'

'Yes. This is the chair lift, isn't it?'

'Er, no. The chair lift is right around the other side.'

'Ah well, never mind, we'll go back and around to the chair lift.'

'Er, the chair lift isa no good.'

'No good?'

'Yes, no good.'

'Why no good?'

'The chair lift isa broken yesterday. It will take twenty days to make it O.K.'

'Chair lift broken, eh?'

'Yes, chair lift broken.'

'Oh.'

'This is the bessa way upa Vesuvio, si si, you go with the car to the end and then isa twenty minute walk to the crater.'

'Twenty minutes?'

'Twenty minutes.'

'Right, then we'll go.'

'O.K. Thatsa 750 lire.'

'All right then, here's 850 lire.'

'750 lire each.'

750 lire each! Those vague black sockets of his somehow

stop me thinking. I feel him suck 1,500 lire out of my hand just like a bug. 1,500 lire to go up a road!

'Right, let's get on then'

'Jussa minute.'

'Now what?'

'You must have a guide.'

'A guide?'

'Yes. You must have a guide to go up Vesuvio.'

'We don't want a guide.'

'Issa forbidden to go up Vesuvio without the guide. Issa very dangerous.'

Suddenly beside him is the guide. Black hair, brown flat face, black glasses. Another bug. The Venetian bats were bad enough but the Vesuvian bugs are worse. In two ticks he's in the car with us. We don't seem to have the power to resist. The bugs have got us. This one sucks 5,000 lire from us. That's his cheapest fee. 5,000 lire! Hahaha, really it's no good when you're on strange territory—you are at an awful disadvantage.

We are as bad as that sad American gentleman we met a few days ago. A very sad and serious American. He came over to us as we sat in a café. He addressed Tubby Foster.

'Excuse me, sir, but are you English?'

'Er yes, thank you, thank you.'

'I have been to your country, sir.'

'Oh, have you? Oh, I see.'

'I am doing a tour of the whole of Europe.'

'Oh, really? Really?'

'Yes sir. I have been badly cheated, sir, in Europe.'

'Oh, cheated.'

'Yes sir. I have been badly cheated in France and very badly cheated in Italy.'

'Not surprised. Not surprised at all.'

'I was very badly cheated in your country, sir.'

'Oh, really? How, where?'

'I was in Cornwall, sir.'

'Oh, Cornwall, yes.'

'Yes sir. I was in Cornwall and I was very badly cheated.'

'How very odd.'

31

'Yes sir. I was in Cornwall, sir, when I met a fisherman, sir, and this fisherman said that for five English pounds he would show me the wreckage of the Spanish Armada.'

'Did he?'

'Yes sir. He told me where to go to see the wreckage of the Spanish Armada.'

'You didn't find it, did you?'

'No sir. I was very badly cheated.'

Very badly cheated, and we secretly laughed at the way the sad American had been cheated. And now we were in almost the same boat. We are being cheated of several thousand lire. We drive up through the vineyards and gorse bushes and then the vegetation dwindles away and up here nothing grows. It's just a black gravel, lava desert, with a rough battered road roaming around it, a cloud of black dust chasing us like a whirlwind. And we arrive at a sort of a shack. This is as far as we can go by car. We walk the rest. The guide leads the way. He doesn't have to—any fool can see which way to go. There's just one path winding up and up.

Suddenly the guide turns as though he's forgotten something. He points to my sandals.

'Sir, those shoes are no good.'

'No good? What's the matter with them?'

'They will get full of little stones and you won't be able to walk.'

'I'll be all right.'

'No, no. Look here, here, here.' And there by the wayside is another bug, and guess what? Yes, you're quite right—he's got lots of pairs of rubber shoes.

'Sir, you must have a pair of these shoes.'

'I mustn't.'

'Sir, for only 500 lire you can hire a pair of shoes.'

'No, I'll go up on my hands and knees. O.K.?'

'O.K.'

He trudges on muttering. I must say I could do with a decent pair of shoes. In sandals it's like walking up a gravel tip. The sandals fill up with agonising little lava stones. Little pumice stones. It's really murder, but I'm not going to let that guide see that I'm in trouble. If you keep kicking out sideways you do get rid of a certain amount of the agony. You can kick the stones out. It takes us about an hour to walk to the crater.

'That fellow down below said it would take just twenty minutes to get to the top,' I mutter.

'I know, but it's no good. We are absolutely in their hands you know, they can do just what they like to us.'

'Yes, I'm afraid so.'

There are quite a few people up at the crater. Some children with their parents go laughing by. Two very old ladies go treading timidly round the rim. They haven't got guides and they didn't come up our way. Obviously the chair lift *isn't* broken down and you *don't* have to have a guide. Walking up Vesuvius at the moment is just about as hazardous as taking a stroll in the Lake District. We have been badly cheated, sir. Oh yes, we've been badly cheated all right. It's a pity because the view from the top of Vesuvius is tremendous. There, just behind us, is the enormous brown burnt crater, a whiff of steam wandering up from it; out there the wonderful bay of Naples and Capri. Down there are the ruins of Pompeii.

It's incredible, it's worth every penny of the small fortune it cost us to get here, but not the way it was extracted from us. But there it can't be helped, for the tourist very often gets the wrong picture of a country. Now if we were to settle and live here for six months or a year then we'd probably find the real Italy. The bats and the bugs would leave us alone, we would get to know the gay lovable Italians and feel at ease in the beautiful landscapes; but as tourists of course we are just fair game for the unscrupulous, easy meat for the dishonest—and of course we don't like it. If you choose to travel about the world instead of staying happily in one place you do make yourself quite vulnerable. Very vulnerable.

CHAPTER THREE

Seeking the Midnight Sun

The tourist is a pretty restless bird. And the more he tours, the more restless he becomes. He's got to keep on the move—if he's in Denmark then he's got to get to Sweden, then from Sweden to Finland and from Finland to Russia. You've just got to get in full flight with other tourists. There's a terrible muddled migration going on all over Europe. We're like a flock of unsatisfied, demented birds fluttering around the capitals of Europe, never roosting properly, sleeping on the wing—you must see as much as the other birds say other birds have seen.

Yeah, well I met a guy yesterday who had come from Florida to New York, New York to Southampton. Then from Southampton he went to London, Paris, Brussels, Amsterdam, then over to Copenhagen, then from Copenhagen . . . 'Yah, yah, zis morning I am speaking viz a man vot is coming from Hamburg and taking ze wessell—zis is right, wessell, yah?—taking a wessell and coming to Plimouse. From Plimouse he is coming to Vales. To Vales (Wales). No, no, to Vales by Bass. By bass (by bus). (To Wales by bus, yes.) No, no, no. To Vales by Bass—zere is a big cassedral bose togesser Bass and Vales. (Bath and Wells, ah yes, yes.) Is so difficult. No, no, no. Zen he is coming to Vimble Eedon. Vimble Eeedon. Vimble Eedon vimbleeedon vimbleedon vimbledon (wimbledon wimble don Wimbledon).'

It's wonderful. We collect pennants for our motor car to show where we have been, our suitcases get battered red and blue with hotel stickers, and we don't remember much about where we've been or what we've seen but by Jingo we've got the evidence and, of course, the pamphlets. Tubby Foster carries a briefcase stuffed full of pamphlets. He is a brilliant pamphlet-snatcher. He can walk beside you through a long hotel foyer, absolutely in step with you. Well, when we get out of the lift he hasn't a pamphlet on him, and yet by the time we get to the hotel front door he's got a half dozen. I don't know how he does it—he is without doubt a most brilliant pamphlet-snatcher. If he really put his mind to it he could graduate to become a very great shop-lifter, but he sticks to the pamphlets, because the pamphlets beguile you, they guide you about, they coax and persuade. Well, look at this one—it shows a most beautiful coloured sunset and in the foreground, in silhouette, a proud reindeer wearing his best hat-rack equipment. What's it say? *Come to the land of the midnight sun where the sun never sets. Come and watch the sun at midnight, toying with the horizon.* Toying with the horizon at midnight. . . .

'That sounds good, doesn't it?'

'Yes, we shouldn't miss that, really. I think we ought to get a move on.'

'But we only arrived in Copenhagen yesterday!'

'Yes, but I don't think we should hang about too much.'

You see, the pamphlets are working their magic spell once again—urging you on and on, all of them saying there are far far better places to see than the place you're in now.

'What's this one say about Copenhagen?' I ask.

'The wisiter can enjoy after the hustle and bustle of the busy city the delights of a stroll by the waterfront at Nyhaven.'

'I wonder where they get this language from?'

'I haven't finished yet!' Tubby snaps.

'Sorry.'

'Zis picturesque situation and colourful hold houses is a spot frequented by artists and sailors alike.'

'Artists and sailors alike—now they've got something there. I always had a job to tell 'em apart.'

'*Please*, I've nearly finished.'

'Sorry.'

'Frequented by artists and sailors alike who mingle with

the wisiters in ze small inns, etc.'

Artists and sailors alike mingle with the visitors. Well, let's have a look at Nyhaven. It's certainly a most pictur-esque situation. Little harbours often are, and this one has got everything. Small ships, bollards, curls of casual rope, old houses, reflections and—look at this—a tattoo shop. The whole place is plastered with snorting Chinese dragons, writhing snakes, flags of all nations, hearts with arrows through them, and all the black-and-blue aboriginal skin engravings that the pagans love. A big notice in the window says: *No pain, no scars*. And through the half-open doorway we can just see a white naked leg being tattooed. No pain, no scars, but a self-inflicted decorated bruise for the rest of your life. Here's another tattoo shop, and another, and here is a small tattoo *ship* with a great notice nailed to the mast—*Tattovering. Tattoverings*. That's a good tatt all over, I suppose. The Danish for tattooing—*tattovering*, huh, because we've already seen lots of signs about *parkering*. Some places you can parkering and some places you can't parkering your car. You can parkering in Nyhaven, all over the harbouring you can parkering, but nosey-parkering or lingering or loitering is not permittering because the whole place is full of the tinkering, the tailoring, soldiering and sailoring, mafek-ing and roistering and staggering. It's quite excitering and there's parkering.

We look around for an inn to parkering and mingling. Well, what about that one? Ready to mingle? It's a desperate sort of a place, a real tin-pot, pick-pocket honky tonk. It looks like a film set. A lot of the characters in here tonight are much too tight to mingle. Two thick-set dirty men with beards and jerseys are talking earnestly together. One is gesticulating madly with his hands and arms. I'm not sure whether he's a sailor telling another sailor how to tie a short sheep-shank in a following wind or an artist telling another artist how he painted his superdoodle—'Two Reclining Figures Looking for a Flea in Bed'. Job to say. In Nyhaven the artists and sailors are very alike. We sit and just watch them and keep very quiet for you could get yourself into a beautiful punch-up here in no time at all. We just watch. Just watching people is a most entertaining pastime.

A couple of days later we arrive at Stockholm and go to a travel agency and ask the young lady to book us a hotel somewhere. While she is phoning around, Tubby Foster and I wander over to the window to watch the people pass. As I say, it's very entertaining and it's free.

'Here's a strange walk,' observes Tubby.

'Mmmmm. Depressed character, I should say.'

'Clerk.'

'No, he looks more to me like a man who works in a cycle shop.'

'Yes, they always look as though they want to be dealing with motor cars.'

'Mmmmm. Course, he's got his saddle set a bit low.'

'Yes, makes him look miserable.'

'Yes. You know, I once knew a man who collected bicycles and he—good heavens, do you see this?'

'Good heavens!'

Huh, you can't miss it. You don't speculate on its character or occupation because it's a woman of sensational beauty. Blonde, beautiful hair, blue eyes deep-set in the head, intelligent, a fine chiselled nose—exquisite. And the way she walks! One beautiful, co-ordinated piece with an easy, swinging rhythm. It's nonsense, it's so perfect. She leaves a sort of vacuum behind her and yet no one in the street takes the slightest notice of her. And you see why. Scarcely ten yards away walks another goddess and another. The whole street is thronging with these dreamlike perfections! It's unbelievable. We watch steadily and then we begin to notice other things about them. They are all carrying shopping baskets—they are housewives and office girls doing their lunchtime shopping! This blonde dream here has just bought a pot-scourer, a cabbage and some cup-hooks for the dresser. It isn't right, really. It isn't right that men should inflict bondage on creatures like this, making them scrape potatoes and wash pots. And, yet, I don't know. There's something slightly peculiar about them—you feel that at any time they are going to be whisked away to the strange spirit world of the mountain mists where the wind whistles through holes in the ice, calling them, calling them. That's what it is. They've all heard something. They've all heard something that we haven't heard, can't hear. Like one of those dog-whistles that send out a very high frequency somewhere beyond here—*wheeeeee!* Have you ever seen a dog called by one of these whistles? His ears go up and then flat to his head, his eyes become suddenly glazed and sightless and he turns and obeys the Svengali call.

Greta Garbo was famous for her dog-whistle look. She used to hear it and even became famous for it. You remember the scene? She's married to a bit of a swine— George—she also has a lover—Henry. She believes that George knows nothing about Henry until one day she is leaving the house when George meets her in the hallway.

'Hello, my dear. Are you going out?'

'Yes I am.'

'Oh, and where are you going, my dear?'

'Oh, just to do some shopping.'

'Oh yes . . . with Henry.' Then she'd get the dog-whistle look. Everything would happen to her face at once, as though some terrible invisible hand had grabbed her hair at the back and twisted it and twisted it, drawing everything tighter and tighter. *Wheee!* Very good. It's a look of controlled terror, mystery, drama and sensitivity.

'Excuse me, but I've managed to get you two rooms.' Of course, if you hear the dog-whistle a lot then you become set.

'Excuse me, but I've managed to get you two rooms.'

Your face takes on this peculiar deep-freeze look.

'*Excuse me*, but I've managed to get you two rooms.'

'What's that?—*whee!* Eh what? *Wheee!* Rooms? (I heard the whistle then.) Rooms—oh good—where?'

'Well, it's not a normal hotel.'

'Oh, what goes on there?'

'Oh no, no, no, no you see it's really a students' hostel, but in the summer it's run as an hotel for visitors.'

'Good, we'll try it.'

It's quite a nice hotel, really. Yes, this will do very well. 'Now what about a drink?'

'Yes, lovely idea—there's the porter.'

'Excuse me, but do you think we might have two gins and something?'

'*Whoo*. I am sorry sir, *whooo*.'

That's always a depressing noise—*whoo*. It not only means they haven't got it, but that you can't get it.

'Er—difficult to get eh?'

'*Whoo* to drink in Sweden for you is hard, so it is.'

'Is it? But I saw places in the city with *bar* written up on them.'

'Yes, but are they only selling cakes and milk and things so it is.'

'Is it? But I also saw a lot of people staggering all over the pavements. Don't tell me that they've all got one leg shorter than the other.'

'No sir, they had been to the *systemboulaget*.'

'The *systemboulaget*?'

'The *systemboulaget*, so it is.'

'What is it?'

'Well sir, huh.'

(I can see that it's very painful for him.) 'Don't hurry. Take your time.'

'Well sir, why it is so, I don't know, so it is.'

So it is. It takes a long time to get a clear picture of the fascinating Swedish drink laws. The English ones by comparison seem rather like a perpetual New Year's Eve. It boils down to this—there are no pubs or bars. Generally, if you want a drink, the only place you can get one is a restaurant where you've got to eat too. Some restaurants are licensed to sell beer, some to sell wine and beer, and some—and this is rather unfair because it always seems to be the most exclusive and expensive ones—some are licensed to sell beer, wine and spirits. So the only way to get a drink and not be forced to eat as well is to buy a bottle at the *systemboulaget*. The *systemboulaget* is a gigantic off-licence and it's government-controlled. There aren't many about because we went looking for one. I don't know why, but we had both suddenly become obsessed with drink.

'Yes, that's the King's palace over the water there—quite nice. Now where is the *systemboulaget*? Yes, that's the Town

Hall along there—that's nice too. Now where is the *systemboulaget*?'

'What's that? There's a queue over there—yes, it's written up over the door, *systemboulaget.*'

'Oh good—now, no need to run!'

We join the queue outside and slowly shuffle in. Queueing for anything is bad enough, but queueing for booze is really rather awful. You begin to feel like a dypsomaniac. Feel like one! There's no doubt about it—you *are* one, otherwise you wouldn't be doing this. The queue moves into the boulaget systematically (I think I can hear the dog-whistles again), and then fans out into four separate queues which lead to a severe counter. It's like a big city post office on Christmas Eve. Six girls behind the counter, flat out, flogging the grog as hard as they can go. Still, it's nice to be together with all the other thousands of dipsomaniacs—as you scuff up for your drug you can look around and be comforted. Well, he drinks and she drinks and he drinks and she drinks. She drinks—pity, lovely girl, too—well you can't help thinking that it has suddenly become a wicked thing to do. Hundreds and thousands of us, all steeped in sin. Poor depraved, weak creatures lining up for Mother's Ruin.

I don't know—have I got a bit of a twitch starting, like that man next to me? He's well on the way! If only I could get rid of the craving—oh gosh I've got to have it! I've got to have it!

'Have what, sir?'

'Eh? Oh a bottle of plin, geeze—er gin, please. Hahahaha! I've got it, come on!'

We scuttle out like two little boys robbing an orchard and smuggle it into our hotel. Don't let the porter see it, tararara! Cor, he nearly caught us, heheheh! Quick—upstairs! Mind you, the *systemboulaget* system was in force when we were over there twenty years ago. Whether it's the same now I really don't know, but there was a time when you were also issued with a card at the *systemboulaget* so that they could mark up your weekly intake—or output, if you like—of liquor.

And then, suddenly, we did it. Perhaps it was the over-civilised Swedish attitude to life that did it (could be), or perhaps it was the pamphlets again.

'What's it say? *Visit the land of the midnight sun, watch the sun toying with the horizon. Visit Finnish Lapland, see the reindeer and the fast-disappearing Lapp.*'

The fast-disappearing Lapp . . . Well, we'd better hurry up or he'll be gone by the time we get there. And so we go off in search of the fast-disappearing Lapp and the sun toying with the horizon. It is not an easy journey. We seem to spend days on country buses bashing along dirt tracks. I have never known country so utterly still. It seems as though it never really gets over being frozen stiff most of the year. The memory of it haunts the dark green fir trees, the silver birches are still, pale and on the point of shivering, and the deep, dark lakes are sombre and thoughtful. We are way up inside the Arctic Circle, and not only are the Lapps fast disappearing but the trees are too, for this is the tundra.

There is a small hotel for those who venture as far north as this—it's quite comfortable but isolated and alone. The main thing is it is somewhere to stay. Accommodation is very scarce up in the tundra, but we are prepared to suffer as long as we get a glimpse of the fast-disappearing Lapp. So far, not a sausage. We've been travelling by bus most of the day and now it's two o'clock in the morning and as light as midday. Very difficult to get to sleep in this perpetual daylight. I feel I've been naughty—it's something like being sent to bed as a child, you don't want to sleep at all.

It doesn't seem to apply just to strangers to the perpetual daylight. You find the natives wandering about at all hours of the night. I'm beginning to long for the dark. What a beautiful drug the dark is—fancy being frightened of the dark! It's your friend, your soothing sleepmaker. It throws a mesh over the senses and lets you drift away. Frightened of the dark! I'm getting a bit frightened of the light.

'Look, it's no good going to bed. Shall we go for a walk?' suggests Tubby. And we go for a walk in the tundra. It's an interesting walk because we keep finding bombs. Yes, quite big bombs, just sort of dropped and not gone off. And look, there's a German helmet and another one and a tangle of barbed wire over there. It seems as though the war finished only last week.

'Here, I don't like this,' said Tubby.

'Like what?'

'Well, I don't suppose they'd ever bother to clear a minefield up here.'

'Eh? You don't think that we are in an old minefield, do you?'

'Well we're certainly on an old battlefield.' Yes, true, all those helmets and bombs. Huh. We both stop dead in the middle of a great big piece of tundra. It's incredible what a little suggestion will do. A few minutes ago we had been walking along happily, but now that Tubby's said 'minefield', we feel surrounded by mines. I'm convinced there's a mine buried just by that old German boot, or a booby trap. I jump over it—it doesn't go off.

'Where's the next one?'

'There, by that tin can—come on, jump it!'

Of course we have both got different ideas where the mines are and jump about all over the shop. We hop and jump all the way to our hotel and don't set off a single mine, but it's one way of tiring yourself out and getting a little sleep.

Now there's a bird in a bush outside my bedroom window. Whistle whistle. He was singing there this afternoon, whistle whistle. He was singing early in the evening, whistle whistle. He was singing at midnight, whistle whistle. Poor little devil doesn't get the benefit of even ten minutes' dark to get a bit of a roost—he's nearly exhausted. Whistle, oh dear, whistle, cough cough, whistle. That's the only way he can get to sleep, too—tire himself out.

The next day we enquire at the hotel reception if there are any fast-disappearing Lapps about.

'Well, not here there are no Lappmen, but I know a taxi-driver who knows where there are some Lappmen. Shall I call him?'

'Yes please.'

The taxi-driver is a jolly sort of a chap who doesn't speak English, and we drive for miles and miles. Not a reindeer or a Lapp in sight. We're back in the pines again and we come to a lively river bouncing around the boulders. A sudden tumble of activity. There's a little house there. The taxi-driver gets out and goes into the house and comes back with a woman. She speaks English.

'You want to find some Lappmen?'

'Yes.'

'Straight on through the forest are living some Lappmen. Perhaps they will put on their clothes for you.'

Put on their clothes for us? Mmm—a sort of striptease in reverse. Sounds exciting. We go on and on and on—and here we are, I suppose. A small log cabin by the side of a lake. A large dog-kennel beside the cabin. There's a large dog having his dinner. He's eating it out of a German helmet. It's rather a macabre picture because it looks as though he's already eaten the rest of the body and is just finishing off the bit under the helmet. The helmet nods and rolls about as he laps and champs inside it. There's an old woman with a bundle of wood coming towards us. An ordinary-looking country woman. The taxi-driver goes over to her and talks to her confidentially. *Oooderpedderingootyapanki*. She nods her head slowly, thoughtfully. The taxi-driver comes back to us. (Mmmm, ya, ya, mmmm.) We must wait.

And then the whole horror of the situation hits us as the old woman goes slowly into her little log cabin. She's going to put her costume on for us—just for us to look at! What have we sunk to? What have we tourists done? We wait outside her verandah. Then the door slowly opens. Papapapapa*pa*! Ladies and gentlemen, introducing for nearly the last time, your friend and mine, the one you've been looking for—the fast-disappearing Lapp! Thank you. Papapapapa*pa*! She hobbles slowly to the front of the verandah, wearing her traditional Lapp costume. It is very colourful, blue and red, trimmed with lace. We can hardly bear to look at her as she stands proudly to attention for a moment or two, her fading eyes scanning the forest for a herd of imaginary reindeer. (The dog's found something to his liking in the German helmet. It slowly shakes its head from side to side.) Then the old Lapp lady turns and walks slowly back indoors. Tararararar! And that's the end of the performance. We feel very nice and ashamed of ourselves. The taxi-driver thinks that about five shillings would be all right for her, so we hand it over and creep away.

One strange thing is that she's on the telephone. In an outlandish place like this. The last Lapp on the telephone. No doubt it's the pamphlet-writers who had it put in for her.

'Hello, Hilda?'

'Yes?'

'Bill here.'

'Oh yes, Bill?'

'Look Hilda, I'm just getting out a pamphlet for next year.'

'Oh yes?'

'You're still there, then?'

'Oh yes.'

'Haven't disappeared then, hahahah! No, well, last year I had you in as the fast-disappearing Lapp, you see. A bit previous, eh? Hahaha! Think you'll hang out all right for a bit—yes? Hahahah! What's that? You've got to go—you've got a carload of tourists coming up the garden path. Ah, you're going to put it on for them, are you eh Hilda? That's the girl, that's the girl. Tara Hilda.'

'Tara Bill, tara.'

The next day we catch a bus and then another bus on our way up to Honnigsvag, the nearest town to the North Cape, where we hope to see the sun toying with the horizon. And—would you believe it?—every bus we get into is full of fast-disappearing Lapps in traditional costume and we pass herds and herds of reindeer. 'Huh, we've been wasting our time, haven't we?' says Tubby.

'Don't, I can't bear to think of that old Lapp lady.'

And we arrive at Honnigsvag. Honnigsvag is a most remote but exciting fishing town and it's always on the move. The whalers and the seal-hunting ships call at Honnigsvag for tins of beans and sheath-knives and the whole place is swashbuckling with sea captains that look like Burt Lancaster after a sticky night out. There are several hotels at Honnigsvag where tourists wait to take the eighteen-mile journey to the North Cape to see the midnight sun, and we wait patiently in one of them. 'Shall we go up tonight or have a good rest and go tomorrow?'

'Let's go tomorrow night, eh?' I suggest.

'Yes.'

'Excuse me, gentlemen, are you going to the North Cape tonight? Perhaps we could share a car—yes?'

'Well, we thought of going tomorrow.'

'Please, gentlemen, listen to me. I have been to ze Norse Cape seventeen times and not ze vonce am I seeing ze midnight sun.'

'Not the once?'

'Not the vonce. Vy?'

'Why?'

'Fog, mist and rain; each year am I coming and staying here some days but never seeing ze midnight sun.'

Well, we'd better go tonight, then. We share a car with the man who's been to see the midnight sun seventeen times and drive towards the North Cape around hard dark mountains, past still blue lakes. It's tremendous and beautiful scenery, and tonight it's clear. Clear and cold. The wind is blowing from the other side of the world. We stand on the great cliffs 1,000 feet above the sea and watch the sun sink slowly down, dropping from left to right, growing redder, hotter. It just touches the sea, seems to struggle there for a few minutes trying not to plunge in, and then it wrenches itself away and climbs slowly back to its own powerful height.

'Well, there we are—we've seen it, we've seen it, we've seen it.'

'Sank gott, sank gott. After ze eighteenth time now I can rest, now I can rest.'

'Perhaps he can, but I doubt it,' mutters Tubby.

So do I. After all, the tourist is a very restless bird. A very restless bird.

CHAPTER FOUR

An Experience of Eastern Inscrutability

There are times when you are not quite sure what is going on. We had such a time in the North Island of Japan. Japan is made up of a lot of islands and the three main ones are Kyushu in the south, Honshu the main island in the middle, and Hokkaido in the north. It's no trouble at all to get to Hokkaido—the screaming jets fly the wild skies over Japan and in a little over an hour after leaving Tokyo we walk down the aluminium staircase from the aircraft and there waiting to meet us is Mr Tazikawa.

We knew he was going to be there, he was to be our guide advisor and as it turned out a very good friend. He speaks pretty good English. 'Ah, Mr Thomas Foster. How do you do? Ah, Mr Johnny Morris. How do you do?' Mr Tazikawa has a beautiful oval face with sad oval eyes and tiny oval ears. Nature was in a fine rhythmic mood when she made Mr Tazikawa because she moulded for him a handsome oval mouth as well. He looks like a mask on a stick, rather like a totem pole. Expressionless and quite inscrutable. But then most eastern faces are inscrutable. Except for laughing, the eastern face hardly moves and you don't know what it's thinking. Inscrutable. What Tubby Foster calls the Scroot.

. . . 'What did they say when you told them we were going to cancel our rooms?'

'Nothing, just gave me the old Scroot, you know.'

'What did they say when you told them that you'd upset the tea all over the floor?'

'Didn't bat an eyelid—just turned the old Scroot on'. . . .

You do not show your emotions. Mr Tazikawa smiled to

begin with, but now he's got the Scroot on—well, he's going
to tell us something and we may not like it so he's got himself
prepared.

'Now gentlemen, I think it would be as well for us to go
straight to your *ryokan*.'

'Oh, you have booked us in, have you?'

'Forgive me, I took the liberty but I think I have chosen
the best place for you, I stay there myself.'

'Well, thank you very much.'

And we drive to the small town of Noboribetsu and to our
ryokan, a Japanese inn. They were built for the convenience of
travellers, not like some of our English inns. It is assumed in
Japan that if you are a traveller then you are bound to have
had a pretty tough time of it. The road has been a difficult
one and a long one. Your load has been heavy. You were
attacked by wild animals, wicked demons haunted you by
night. You were set upon by brigands and beaten merci-
lessly, your horse was stolen, your belongings filched and
your money taken. Well, not quite all your money otherwise
you wouldn't be able to pay your bill at the *ryokan*. Anyway,
that is the sort of state in which the landlord of a *ryokan*
expects to find his guests when they arrive, because the
moment you appear he is at the door with his wife and
children all bowing. Quick, quick, quick, call the servant
girls! The servant girls, all dressed in kimonos, come
shuffling at the double-shuffle. They grab our bags. Oh no,
these suitcases are much too heavy for these fragile little bits
of porcelain. No, no, no, a big fourteen-stone man might
strain something lifting a hundredweight and a half like that.
These girls are so slight they have nothing to strain. Go on,
shooo, off you go, girls.

The girls go struggling off in the same sort of desperate
way that ants do when they move their eggs over knobbly
ground. We follow them.

'Bit of a cad, aren't you, letting those poor little girls hump
your gear?'

'It's shaming, isn't it? Hey, whoa! Shoes!'

'Oh yes, shoes.'

There is a point in the entrance to a *ryokan* beyond which

you must not go without taking off your shoes. There's a very good reason for this—the Japanese do not have chairs. You sit on the floor; you have your meals sitting on the floor; you live on the floor, you sleep on the floor and so the floor must be kept spotlessly clean. To walk into your room in street shoes is just about the most revolting thing that you can do. It's like walking all over the best velvet-covered settee in gum boots. You wouldn't dream of doing so, it's barbaric.

We take off our shoes and pad along the corridor in lightweight slippers provided by the landlord, and when we reach our rooms these slippers are slipped off and we shuffle the shiny rush matting in socks. Mr Tazikawa has a room next to the room that has been booked for Tubby Foster and myself. It's a simple lovely room with delicate sliding doors covered in opaque paper, one vase in an alcove with a large twig in it, one picture of a kingfisher, one small low lacquered table in the centre of the room, four cushions to sit on, one minute dressing table (you've got to sit on the floor to see yourself in the mirror) and two substantial bits of furniture: a television set and a refrigerator. The fridge is stocked with whisky, gin, beer, tomato juice and squash.

'That's handy.'

'Yes, no need to trouble the night porter.'

'Hi.' Who's that? 'Hi.' Oh it's a serving maid. 'Hi, Hi.' She's holding in her arms a neat pile of, er, sheets and blankets or something, I suppose. 'Hi.' She puts them on the floor, slops over to me and shakes the lapel of my jacket. '*Ekunabashi.*' What's the matter? '*Ekunabashi.*' She does it again. She wants me to take my jacket off. All right then, how's that? 'Hi. Hi.' Then she shakes my shirt and tie. She wants them too. Well, all right then. 'Hi. Hi.' She goes to the pile of blankets and comes back with a sheet and a blanket—oh, but it's not, the sheet unfolds into a cotton robe. Put it on. 'Hi.' The blanket turns itself into a woollen robe with loose pouchy sleeves. Now this. 'Hi.' All right. 'Hi.' She shakes my trousers. You want these? 'Hi.' *Hey*! 'Hi.' All right, I'm powerless.

'Well, what do you think of that?'

'If you don't mind me saying so old man, you really do

look a bit of a nana.'

'Well, it's your turn now.' And Tubby Foster is made to change his Western clothes for Eastern ones. These clothes are provided by the *ryokan*, and they all seem to be uniform, although we are told different *ryokans* have different uniforms.

'Well, how does that look then?'

'Tubby, it's an incredible transformation. Do you know, you look very much like Mrs Pankhurst.'

'Hi.' Oh, the serving maid with tea. Whatever time of the day you arrive at a *ryokan* you are given clean clothes and tea is served at once. There's nothing for it but to sit on the floor with your legs tucked underneath you—oh my goodness, it's *agony*—and take tea. It's green tea, thin, bitter and strange.

' 'Ere, what do they call this?'

'Tea.'

'Cor. There're no handles on the cups.'

'No, it helps you to show off your hands, I suppose. Instead of hooking your great finger in the handle you hold the cup with two hands like a flower holding the gentle raindrops.'

'Well, I think it's a bit odd.'

Come to think of it the whole situation is odd. Here we are sitting on the floor, dressed in robes, drinking tea out of cups with no handles; it's a bit like being in a genteel asylum for mild madmen. And they've got us safely inside. I feel that if ever I become mentally unbalanced I'm sure it will be like this. You see they won't try to force me to go in the bin, no that's the wrong way to do it, they'll see the doctors and the magistrates and get everything signed and trick me in—just like this—and make everything appear to be normal when it isn't.

And they'll agree with everything I say: 'I'm not mad, you know.'

'Of course you're not.'

'No, well I'm not, that's all.'

'Of *course* not.'

And they'll slyly take things away from me so that I can't escape.

'Where're my trousers? Tubby, where're my trousers!'

'I don't know, she took them with mine.'

'Well, I want them back!'

'What for?'

'I'm not mad, you know.'

''Course you aren't.'

There you are, they're saying it. I don't like being without my trousers. The psychological effect of losing your trousers forever is greater than you may think. You are basically insecure; you have literally been undermined.

Mr Tazikawa comes slipping around the sliding doors, a lovely oval smile rippling around his oval face. 'I trust gentlemen that you are comfortable?'

It's agony sitting like this actually, but I say: 'Oh yes, fine!'

'Yes, fine!' Tubby echoes.

'You have enjoyed your tea?'

It was awful really but we say: 'Yes, fine!'

'Excellent! Now gentlemen, when you are ready it is customary to take a bath.'

'Oh, yes?'

'You probably know that the bath in the *ryokan* is a communal bath.'

'Communal?'

'Communal.'

'That means all together, doesn't it?'

'All together.'

'Men and women?'

'Men and women.'

Tubby Foster's face is a study of awe and astonishment. He can't manage to get any Scroot going at all.

Mr Tazikawa turns to him: 'Mr Foster, you take a bath?'

Tubby's a brave man, but this is a bit much for him. He blushes and stammers: 'Er . . . er . . . I might, I might.' Well done, Tubby; you can't catch him out!

'Right gentlemen, I will show you the way.'

We follow Mr Tazikawa to the communal bath. What are we doing? What's going on?

'I'm not mad, you know.'

'Of course you aren't,' Tubby reassures me.

But I'm not far off it. Not so long ago I was in my garden in England, *with* my trousers on, harvesting my shallots and listening to the robin rolling out his little river of song. I was happy then—why did I give up the old life? You have these thoughts as you walk to your execution. Well, you'd think we were going to be executed as we tramp in our robes down the long, long corridor, each man, as they say, alone with his thoughts. Still, you're not alone with them for long because you've soon got other things to think about.

We arrive at the communal bath. There is a changing room for men and a separate one for women. The men's changing room is a large well-proportioned room full of Japanese gentlemen changing from something into absolutely nothing. If that's the way it is, never let it be said we funked it, right? One, two, three: we let our robes slip. Mmm, not a bad specimen of Englishmen, I must say. The Japanese gentlemen find us very interesting—Hmmm, they are sneaking slitty looks at us from all over the room. It's the sensational whiteness of our skins that they seem to find interesting. Hmmm, haw; there's no doubt about it, we certainly wash much whiter.

'Right, gentlemen, the bath is through those doors and you might like these.' Mr Tazikawa hands us each a small towel the size of a lady's handkerchief. 'That you will find useful for—er—wiping away perspiration and for—eh, hahah.'

'Oh, I see.'

Well, that's very dainty I must say. You just hold the pocket handkerchief in front of you as nonchalantly as possible, as though you didn't really care if you had it or not. After a while you get as skilful as a fan dancer with your pocket handkerchief.

We go into the bathroom. It's more of a bath palace really. The main bath is a tremendous circular cauldron about thirty feet in diameter, with a statue in the middle. Three life-size, demure stone nymphs are poised above the water, and sticking out of the steaming water are lots of Japanese faces. The ones with their hair done up in buns on the top are ladies and they've got the Scroot on. But even through the Scroot I can see they find us interesting. Just then two young ladies walk right past us looking as they did when they were born, only bigger and more attractive. I think I'm going mad. I've felt like that for some little time now . . .

Come on, let's get on with the bath. Now, you do not wash yourself in the bath at all. What, wash all the dirt off yourself and then soak in it? Oh, what a filthy thing to do. So you wash yourself at the side of the bath first of all—that's what all those taps are for around the wall. You take a little blue plastic bowl and one of these daft little wooden stools and find a spare tap. There's one—between that largish Japanese lady and that young Japanese gentleman. They are both squatting on stools. I saunter up as casually as I can, carrying bowl and stool in one hand and my handkerchief in the other. I feel like some daft sort of nightclub act. I'm sure I could do it better to music. *Tararara.* I put the stool on the floor and the bowl under the tap, *tarararara*. Now, is anyone looking? *Tararara.* Well, I'm sure there's going to be trouble. That little stool is actually the size of a postcard and now it's on the floor; way down there it looks about as big as a postage stamp. I'll never land on that. And once you start to descend you're flying blind, you can't see where you'll touch down, *tararara*, come on, alle oop, *drrrrrrrrpangbong*: missed! I just catch the back edge of the stool. It tips over backwards, and so do I. I make a noise like a fat halibut being thrown on a fishmonger's slab and I'm sprawled flat on my back. It's fairly undignified to be without your clothes in any case, but making an exhibition of yourself like this is absolutely ghastly. You'd go to prison for doing this in England in public.

For a few seconds I feel like getting up and belting off as fast as I can. But it's surprising how quickly you adapt to fresh conditions. As far as I can see nobody is taking the slightest notice of my antics, although it's a bit of a job to tell. All those faces sticking out of the hot water there, they are all immobile with the Scroot turned full on. No one knows what anyone's thinking. I manage to crawl on to my stool and get on with the washing.

And oddly enough in about a minute I feel quite composed. The Japanese lady next to me is a most thorough washer. She's like a big pussy cat the way she keeps on and on cleaning, cleaning. Surely she's finished now? No, she's not satisfied with her back and so a friend of hers gives her back a good scrubbing. I feel so confident now I almost ask her to do mine for me, but I can't speak the language and so I leave it, swill off all the soap suds and go to the big bath.

It's a most beautiful affair, with ledges all around. You choose which ledge you like to sit on according to how deeply you want to be immersed.

'How are you getting on then?'

'Oh fancy meeting you, Johnny, well, well, well. Got much on these days? Hahaha.'

We sit and soak with just our heads sticking out of the water. Sitting soaking next to us are two ladies chattering away. One finds the water a little on the hot side and she sits on the top ledge with just her feet submerged. She's talking about something pretty important. I wonder what it is? . . .

'Well, I didn't know what to do, *really*, I mean there was this pink kimono and this blue one, you know, but I never think I look my best in blue—' . . .

No, you look jolly nice as you are. Why dress up? A few minutes ago I thought we were in a sort of madhouse. Now I feel almost sure that this is sanity and the other life madness. A whole family of nude Japanese come in for a wash and a soak. Mum, Dad and all the kids. You know one of the nicest things to do, I always thought, was to sit in a street café in Seville and just watch the people stroll by in their finery, but this has got that licked, hasn't it? Mmmm, soon get used to being like this, don't you. Mmmm, doesn't take a minute. We sit naked and unashamed with dozens of other fellow beings.

'I find people fascinating, don't you?'

'Yes, absolutely fascinating.'

And there are some very fascinating people in the northern island of Hokkaido. The next day we go to have a look at them. Everybody goes to have a look at them. They come from all over Japan to look at them. In coaches, trains and aeroplanes they all come to look at the Hairy Ainu. The Hairy Ainu are a race of people who are only found in any numbers in the northern island of Japan. They are not Japanese, and it's a bit of a mystery where they come from. They have a different language and they are hairy, which in these parts is unusual as the Japanese, generally speaking, are not a very hairy nation, so the Hairy Ainu are something of an oddity. They are only about as Hairy as the hairy European and they let their beards grow big and bushy— well, they *used* to, but nowadays they shave so how you tell what is Ainu and what isn't Ainu I don't know. They also tattoo their womenfolk around the mouth. Well, they used to but not now. The tattooing was a mark of possession to show that the lady was married, so any girl who looks as though she's been eating blackcurrant pie you leave alone.

Mr Tazikawa gives us this information about the Hairy Ainu as we drive to one of their villages on the coast not far from Noboribetsu.

'It's nice to be in Western clothes again, isn't it, Tubby.'

'Yes, I really missed my trousers, you know.'

'So did I, but I'm quite looking forward to the peace and tranquillity of the Japanese inn again; this is the way to live you know, you get the best of both worlds.'

'Yes, are you going to have a bath again tonight?'

'Wouldn't be surprised . . .'

Here we are, this must be it. It's a scattered village of wooden huts by a windy, sunny shore. Here live these primitive people and they've all got television aerials on their lashed-up shacks. Of course, Japanese and Ainu live here and since the Ainus now shave it's a job to tell which is which.

'Mr Tazikawa, is that one?'

'I think perhaps yes.'

'Is that one?'

'Er—probably not.'

'Is that?'

'Mmmmm . . .'

But that's one. No mistaking him, standing in the village square, a benign figure with a big beard like a thundercloud.

He's wearing robes, a sword and a strange crown of straw; he's bowing, bidding us welcome. 'Come, please come.' No wonder, he runs the biggest souvenir shop in town. In fact the whole square is a jumble of souvenir shops—souvenir shops mostly selling carved bears.

The Ainu and bears have a strange relationship. The Ainu believe that bears are spiritual messengers and when the bears die they carry messages from this world to the world of the Gods. So to keep well in with the Gods the Ainu take a baby bear, and it is suckled by one of the Ainu women. It is brought up as one of the family until it is three years old, when it is big enough to take its message to the Gods. Well, of course it has to be killed to release its soul first of all. That's a pity, but the bear will then deliver to the Gods a sort of progress report on the Ainu—they are doing all right, they say their prayers, they are kind and gentle (after all, wasn't the bear reared on human milk) and now please can the bear go back to earth in the shape of another bear. Thank you.

And so we all buy a small pocket-size bear from the Ainu. There are only two obvious Ainus in the village, this one with the shop and one fast asleep on a bench. And all the time we are there the coaches come bowling in, spilling out Japanese tourists. The Japanese are great sightseers and trippers, they like to be photographed standing beside a Hairy Ainu. They hire Ainu costumes to be photographed in—you can even hire false, Hairy Ainu beards to go with them—and the souvenir bears sell like hot cakes. How silly of us, we thought that nobody much would be interested in the Hairy Ainu. It just goes to show the Japanese are as interested in their own country as we are.

We follow the coaches back to the next great sightseeing location: the Valley of Hell. The Valley of Hell is quite spectacular. It's a tremendous crater, a vast jagged bowl, and it's full of steam. From the distance it's like a big dish of boiling porridge. And that's roughly what it is. This is the land of volcanoes, tidal waves, earth tremors, hot springs, boiling mud. The earth's skin is very thin and unhealthy here, it suppurates and oozes quite a bit. The Valley of Hell is a very old carbuncle—a nasty, unsafety valve for the world's unattractive poisons. You can smell them here, sniff strong subterranean sulphur.

'Mr Johnny Morris, you like to go down? There is no charge.'

'Mr Tazikawa, is it safe?'

'Mr Johnny Morris, the notice here says it can be dangerous. You must use your common sense.'

Now this is a nice approach to life. We live in a world where people are always saying that all sorts of things oughtn't to be allowed. And they're always the wrong things. Here things are allowed. We walk down into the swirling steam. Can't see where it's coming from—oh yes, there. It's just a hole in a hump in the ground, and shooting from it is a fierce hissing of steam like a railway engine at bay. There's another one, quite a big one!

'Mr Tazikawa, is that the one?'

'Mr Johnny Morris, that is the one.'

That's the hole that people jump down to a glorious suicide. There's another hole and another all spurting steam . . . there's enough steam here to drive a power station.

Let's go a bit further. I steady my hand on a rock—*deeeee*, look at that, a tiny hole in the rock the size of a kettle spout, merrily boiling away! The ground is hollow and the rocks are hollow, and all the scenery is made of papier mâché and pie crust. We come to a boiling stream that leads to a boiling lake, its banks are a slurry of boiling mud that chortles with a devilish glee, glugglegulgglug. I can feel a stupid, foolhardy feeling coming on.

'You know, people like you ought not to be allowed down here.'

'Oh shut up, Tubby.'

'Hi. Hi!'

'Who's that?' Oh, up there on top of that cliff a man is calling. He's a Japanese. I can only see his face, it looks quite ghostly in the steam.

'Hi! Hi! Come come.'

'Mr Johnny Morris,' Mr Tazikawa says, 'he wants us to go up.'

'A busybody, I expect.'

'Let's go up,' urges Tubby.

'All right.' We go up and Mr Tazikawa talks to the face in the steam. He is not interfering, he wants to help. He's a guide who knows the place well. He is not asking for business, but merely wants to tell us that last week three people went through the papier mâché where we were, and they're still in hospital with scalds and burns. For our own sakes he will show us for nothing a place where we can view the boiling mud in safety.

We follow him through the steam for about half a mile and come to a stream. It's a cold stream, only a few feet wide, that flows down into hell from the cool mountains. The guide jumps it, and lands on the pie crust on the other side; it crumbles and he disappears up to his knees in boiling mud. He reacts like a cat: *Meeeeaaaaw*! He shoots into the air and lands back on our side of the stream.

We help him off with his shoes and socks—one leg is not too bad but the other is quite badly burned. No, he says, it is nothing. It was his fault, he was taking a short cut he shouldn't have.

That leg must be agony. I look at his face. You wouldn't know he was in pain. He's got the Scroot full on. No, he will not be carried, thank you. If we will excuse him he will call at the hospital. And standing on one leg in agony, his face a complete blank, he bows to us and hops away into the steam with controlled dignity.

I look at Mr Tazikawa. He's watching the hopping guide disappear into the steam. No way of reading his thoughts. When we leave Hokkaido we give Mr Tazikawa a bottle of whisky. He is delighted with it and sorry that we are going, but that reaction lasts for one-fifth of a second, then, he's a mask on a stick again. Control fighting emotion. You can almost hear pistons of emotion pumping away inside him—his face doesn't move but it's having a terrible battle with itself. He's really into full Scroot now.

As I say, sometimes in Japan you just don't know what's going on, and sometimes you *almost* do.

CHAPTER FIVE

The Lure of the Amethysts

When you are lucky enough to be able to travel around the world the least you can do, the very least you can do is to bring back presents for the ones who were not so fortunate and had to stay at home. It's not much to expect of us, I know—just a little souvenir from here and there. But to find something that doesn't weigh too much, and doesn't cost too much, and doesn't look too awful *and* isn't the same as the one you took back last year—well, it isn't easy.

And there are certain parts of this world where presents are not funny at all. I'll never forget in Africa having to decide between a hippopotamus foot turned into an ashtray, the back leg of a Thompson gazelle turned into a bedside lamp, half a zebra turned into a fireside pouf and a Ghurka's disembowelling knife or whatever it is. I was forced to bring back the disembowelling knife, and the recipient didn't think much of that, I can tell you. Well, I had to bring back *something*.

And now the time has come once again to think about things to take back home. We sit in our bedroom in Rio, Tubby Foster and I, brooding a bit.

'It's no use—we've got to go out into Rio again and face up to it.'

'Yes I know.'

I can't say that we have grown to love Rio. Now pretty well everybody knows what Rio de Janeiro looks like. It is a sensational-looking city from above—a cluster of conical rock mountains bubbling up beside the sea, and scrambling all around the mountains are ten million assorted buildings, from shining skyscrapers to cardboard shacks. It's not really a city at all, it's a landscape with buildings. A scenic city, if you like, and the only way to look at it is from one of the mountains, as if it was a fantastic chunk of scenery. But once you get away from the landscape and down amongst the buildings you find yourself in as dismal a dump as you would find anywhere. Rio doesn't stand up to a very close inspection. It looks fine on a postcard from the sea, but the best and most popular place in it is the Corcovada, the Hunchback. The Hunchback is the name given to one of the vertical mountains around which Rio is built, and on top of the Hunchback stands the tremendous concrete statue of Christ, with its arms outstretched high above the city. It was meant to be gigantic and impressive and it certainly is gigantic and impressive. Wherever you are in the city you can't help just glancing in its direction now and again to see if it's there and hasn't fallen down, because it seems to be just balancing there with its arms out as though walking a tight rope. Some people say they have seen it wobble. Others say that when the Corcovada is enveloped in clouds Christ lowers his arms and takes a breather.

But he certainly looks down on a beautiful muddle of a city, and no doubt the people who live in the favellas look up to him from time to time for a little hope. Because there's little to be hopeful about in the favellas. The favellas are the slums. In fact, according to this pamphlet lying on the reception desk they form part of a motor coach tour. Tour No. 3 of the City of Rio, visiting the Sugar Loaf, the Corcovada and the slums. It means they are worth taking a look at.

And indeed they are—for several different reasons. By visiting these slums you can assess the limits of human endurance and calculate the degree of fortune that blesses some and curses others. The favellas are not slums as we know them—a part of a city where the old properties have become dilapidated and tumbledown. Oh no, these slums are all hand-made, do-it-yourself jobs. They are not old buildings, they're new and they're building them all over the place and they're *awful*.

59

The basic cause of a slum is, I suppose, too many people and not enough money. Governments are supposed to attend to such problems and if they don't ordinary human beings in desperation will deal with them themselves. And they've done this in Rio—individuals have built themselves somewhere to live. Bonk! Like that. And about a quarter of a million individuals live in the favellas, so it's said.

How did they do it? Where did they find the land? Well, Rio is a unique city. I've already said it's a landscape with buildings, an eruption of steep rocky mountains with the buildings clambering as high as they can up the rock face. Now there comes a point when a rock face is too steep to make normal building practical or economical and so for years these rock faces have gazed over Rio, vacant and bare. But desperation is an urgent and inventive spur. The homeless found that if you could drive a couple of poles into the steep mountainside you could make yourself a platform. And once you've got a platform you can easily put a roof on it. There's plenty of material knocking about—wood packing cases, corrugated iron. Of course you've got to hack the rock here and there to get a toe hold, but you can cut steps and recesses and you don't need a lot of room.

And so these incredible battered and cobbled wooden shackeries have grown up and up all over the hillsides of Rio, like great colonies of sea birds perched high on the cliffs, and like sea birds they nest and breed and have no alternative but to endure in the filth they make themselves. But like sea birds they have the best views of all. The great city of Rio, the vast beaches, the roaring rolling seas, you see all this from your little hutch in the favella. You'd pay £20,000 a year for a flat with a view like this and you can live here for nothing.

Of course, you're not supposed to be here. Oh no, the law is quite definite about this: squatting is not allowed and everybody knows that. Who cares? The people who made the laws cannot possibly enforce them and the favellas spread bigger and higher. Wonderful, do-it-yourself, un-planned huggermuggers bursting with individuality.

We ventured into a favella the other day. We were told that it wasn't advisable.

'But it seems all right, doesn't it?'

'Yes, the people seem friendly enough.'

We climb the steep steps between the rickety shacks. The ingenuity of the amateur shack-makers is astonishing, they'd knock up a shack on the side of the Post Office tower. And they are complete little homes—dogs loll about on tiny balconies inches wide, kids play up and down the steps, women hang out their bits of grey washing. An incredibly smart young girl comes out of a ghastly old shack just in front of us and goes off down the steps towards the main road below.

'Honestly, you wouldn't know,' I say.

'You would not know,' Tubby agrees.

She looks as though she might have walked out of the Hilton Hotel, not from an unidentified rabbit hutch in the favella. It's an astonishing place. We follow a tiny goat track between the packing cases no more than eighteen inches wide and we come to a small square about twelve feet by twelve feet where there is a little general store selling groceries and soft drinks. There's a woman leaning over the half door.

'Good afternoon.'

'Oh! Good afternoon; you knew we were English?'

'I heard you talking. I was once in England. I come from Poland,' she replies.

There are a thousand questions you feel you should ask her right away. But you can't. She saves us the embarrassment.

'Don't go any higher.'

'Don't go any higher?'

'No.'

'Oh.'

'It is not safe.'

'Not safe?'

'No.'

She taps my watch with her forefinger and then sweeps it across her throat. 'Oh.'

'It is a long way to escape to the road, and the sun is going down,' she says.

'Yes, I see. Thank you.'

We take her advice and go no higher. Well, there are many here who have nothing and they are inclined to envy those who have something.

And it was while we were walking back from the favella that we chanced upon this strange shop. Well, it was strange to us.

'What's that in the window?'

'It's a lump of quartz, isn't it?' I said.

'Yes, fantastic stuff isn't it?'

Yes. The entire window space of this little shop is filled with lumps of stone, as big as footballs some of them. Pale pink, deep amber, sinister green, passionate purple, we gaze at these elusive colours that shimmer from the lumps of rock, and I suppose it was then that we were taken over. The mysterious influence from the red-hot past took possession of us, the evil demon who lives in the bowels of the earth, where these stones were blasted in blinding white heat, had got us. We were hooked and we didn't know it. I might have heard a high whine in my head, I'm not sure (*waawaawaawaawaa*).

'Good evening, gentlemen. Two gentlemen from England, hahaha, what can I do for you?'

Hey, how did we get in here—we are in the shop! We had no reason to come into the shop, we don't want to buy lumps of coloured rock!

'Please take your time, have a look round, I'm sure it will interest you,' the owner says. He's got an overpowering face, like a lizard with glasses on, and a small trilby hat. It's the sort of face that you'd run a mile from but his lizard eyes are mild and still, pale yellow eyes with a tiny black dot in the middle of each one. He's not smiling but he seems to be. He pouts in a very unpleasant way, his tight thin lips smirking around his face like the zip fastener of an overstuffed handbag. He rests his little lizard hands on the top of the glass counter, tiny hands turned in, pigeon fingered. Just like a lizard on a rock (*waawaawaawaa*).

'Do take your time, gentlemen, do take your time.'

'Thank you, we were just . . . you know, not very interested really, just . . . *waawaawaawaawaa*.'

'Take your time please, take your time.'

'Thank you.'

'Thank you.'

The shelves of his shop are loaded with lumps of crystal and quartz, milky quartz, rose quartz, green quartz, smoky quartz, aquamarine, beryl, garnet, black tourmaline, jasper, agate and feldspar. They must dig this stuff up by the ton. Yes, look, they make things out of it—ashtrays, paperweights, little dishes for putting things in.

'These things are not important, gentlemen, they are for the tourist, cheap things for the tourist. I can show you other things, things a little more serious.' He holds up in his little warty paw a soft leather pouch. 'Would you like to see what is in here?' His other warty paw smooths a piece of black velvet on the counter, and like a little reptile conjurer he shoots the leather pouch across the velvet, suddenly checks it and a startling cartwheel of pale blue light spills, tumbles and glitters about the velvet. We are riveted. The spinning stones, so instantly stilled, wallow in the white electric light and flicker it back pale blue. There lie about twenty aquamarines, the most beautiful aquamarines.

'You like to look to this one?' He puts an aquamarine as big as a cob nut in my hand.

'That is quite a nice one.'

'Yes, isn't it.' It is of the palest and yet the darkest blue, if you see what I mean. You can look into it down into the deep blue sea. It's fifty fathoms deep and the size of a nut. I want it, I want it! I want this beautiful stone. What for? I don't know. I want it, I want it!

'This is a better one—you see, it is darker.' He puts another one in my hand. Yes, it's darker, a deep aquamarine. It's glorious, wonderful! I want it, I want it!

'Now this one is bigger, but it has a little imperfection—here—that would be much cheaper; but this one is my favourite, I think.' He pushes forward with a little lizard finger an aquamarine the size of a small walnut. It knows it's the best one of the bunch, and it just lies naked and unashamed on the black velvet winking with blue light. A crystallised giant splash of the mighty sea.

We are both absolutely fascinated. I look up and get a glimpse of the lizard watching us. But his yellow eyes flick away in an instant and pick out a lump of rose quartz on a distant shelf. He knows he's got us. Well, look at us! We are grovelling like savages over an explorer's glass beads. No wonder poor innocent aborigines gave up their lands and possessions for a handful of coloured glass stones. I almost believe that I would do the same. If the lizard said to me, 'You can have these aquamarines if you will give me your house and garden and furniture and motor car, will you do that? Will you, will you?' Yes I'll do that, I'll do that!

But he doesn't ask me, he simply rakes the aquamarines back into the soft leather pouch with his warty paws.

'Very beautiful stones aquamarines, *very* beautiful,' he says.

'Yes, very—*very*.'

My pulse is banging away at quite a rate. Well, I was on the verge of selling goodness only knows what, for just one of those aquamarines. My emotion wants me to buy the aquamarines regardless of everything; my scrap of intelligence tells me not to be a twit, don't do it. Yes? No. Yes? No. The lizard has only to give me the slightest push and I'll be committed. But he doesn't. He lets me off the hook, he lets both of us off the hook!

He says, 'Well, gentlemen, perhaps you will drop by again when you are passing eh?'

'Yes, of course.'

'Yes, I expect so, haahahaha.'

We blunder out into the street.

'Phew, I say Tubby, what a relief to be out here.'

'Yes, isn't it?'

'It's as though some spell has been lifted.'

'You know, I was on the point of going mad in there?'

'So was I! I was thinking about flogging the camera or my wrist watch.'

'I know. These stones are something, aren't they? We mustn't go back in there again.'

'Not on your nellie.'

But the very next evening, on our way home—

waawaawaawaawaa, we're back in with the lizard again. This time he's got a leather pouch full of amethysts. He doesn't press us to buy. There's no difficulty about leaving his shop empty-handed.

'You know, I've just realised what he's up to!'

'So have I, he's educating us,' said Tubby.

'Yes, he's *educating* us. Clever little lizard. He's making sure we will appreciate the best and only buy the best. He knows we are going to buy something, and you do learn very quickly to tell a good aquamarine from an indifferent aquamarine. He's in no hurry. ('Take your time gentlemen, please take your time.') Well, we'll see what happens tonight.

Wawawaaaaawaaawaaa . . . 'What would you like to see tonight, gentlemen? Oh, some amethysts. Ah, I got some nice new amethysts this morning, you haven't seen these before.' He tumbles them out of the soft leather pouch. 'Now which one do you like?'

'Er, this one.'

'Yes, very good, very good. This one would be the best, you are right it *would* be the best but it has here one small imperfection, you see?'

'Ah yes, pity.'

'Yes, but never mind, we learn a little every day—every day a little more?' the lizard reassures.

We go over the amethysts one by one and before he scoops them back into the pouch he flickers a quick yellow look at us. No, we're not ready—not yet. Back go the amethysts into the pouch.

'So, perhaps you will drop by again, gentlemen?'

'Well, we are leaving Rio tonight.'

'Tonight?'

'Tonight.'

Reptiles are not very emotional creatures as far as we know. They demonstrate their anger of course, and their warning to keep away. Some lizards stiffen their leather neck-frills and some snakes shake a rattle in their tails or spread a hood around their necks. Often a little newt will flap his gullet and that can mean *anything*. That's all the lizard with the glasses and the trilby does—he flaps his gullet twice. He's missed us, after all that careful watching and judging he's missed us!

'You're leaving tonight?'

'Yes.'

'Where do you go?'

'To Brasilia.'

'To Brasilia and then?'

'Back to Rio.'

'Back to Rio?'

'Back to Rio.' He knows he hasn't missed us.

'Have a nice trip, gentlemen, have a nice trip. Perhaps you will drop by again?'

Perhaps we will, perhaps we will. Perhaps when we get to Brasilia the spell will be broken and we will have forgotten all about those devilish bits of glass.

And we almost forget about the bits of glass because Brasilia takes quite a bit of looking at. The idea of building a capital city away from the coast, away from Rio, was first mooted as long ago as 1789. One government after another thought about it, made a few suggestions, turned them all down and left it to the next government to kick about a bit. After all, what's the point of building a new capital city something like a thousand miles from the coast, where nobody and nothing lives save a few Indians and a bunch of twisted rattlesnakes? It's barmy, there's nobody there. Ninety-three per cent of the population of Brazil is firmly settled on the coast, in cities like Rio and San Paulo. Hardly anyone lives in the interior.

But the idea of having something new is irresistible to individuals and to governments. It was said, you see, that if a new capital were built in the interior it would open the country up, and heaven knows it needs opening up! And so this idea niggled on and on until, almost out of sheer irritation it seems, the Brazilian government decided to build Brasilia.

There were no roads leading to the jungle site and so the building materials were flown in. Yes, flown in. Steel, cement, bricks, mortar—enough to start the city. And so began the most grandiose building operation since the pyramids, I imagine. Dams were built where several rivers converged, and a tremendous lake was formed. You need water to reflect the beautiful buildings (architects do so love an encore). You need water to reflect the perfect plan for a lovely life. It's a beautiful example of authority saying: 'This is how you *will* live,' and not: 'This is how we *think* you might like to live.' The arrogance of planners, the skill of engineers and the strange way of architects have all pulled together and against one another in forcing this artificial monument out of the ground.

We heard all sorts of stories about Brasilia before we went there:

'You're going to Brasilia? Oh good heavens, what a dump! One day there is enough. You'll go mad, you know. They can't get anybody to stay there. Do you know what the government had to do to get the officials to go and live there? They had to give them free flats to live in, free motor cars, and no taxes to pay! It's true, well it's like asking people to go into exile. To prison for life. You'll see, you will soon be back in Rio. The government was mad to build it!'

Well, perhaps it was. It certainly went on one of the biggest building-spending sprees of this century. And when you go on a spending spree you're sure to acquire a few things that are worthwhile no matter how reckless you've been. And there are some things in Brasilia that are certainly worthwhile.

We are taken around them the morning after we arrive by a very nice guide with a very nice motor car and a perfectly painful voice: 'And now gentlemen, we will start the day in our beautiful new city of Brasilia by explaining that this is the centre of government. All government affairs are dealt with here in Brasilia. The government officials are housed in these blocks of flats which are described as neighbourhoods. They are self-contained, having in them their own markets, hospitals, churches, schools and shops.' The neighbourhoods are just lumps of square buildings standing beside the main avenue that runs through Brasilia. 'Now gentlemen, I have given you the neighbourhoods, I will now give you the different ministries: the Ministry of Agriculture, the Ministry for the Army, and so on. First of all I give you, to the left, the Ministry of Agriculture.' He introduces his buildings as though they were cabaret acts or heavyweight boxers.

'I think we ought to give him a round of applause when he gives us the next building, don't you?' I whisper.

'Wonder if he'd appreciate it?'

'And now gentlemen, I give you, to the left, the Ministry of Housing.'

They are all rectangular buildings set in lawns and gardens. There's bags of room everywhere. There are great open areas of grass and creeping plants. There are swimming pools and race tracks, airfields for real aeroplanes and airfields for model aeroplanes. The whole city is set in the open countryside—it must look wonderful on paper and it is wonderful from the top of the television tower, like an enormous half-empty cemetery waiting for an epidemic. The avenues are generously wide and extravagantly long. Nothing is cramped, everything is spread out. Well, there's so much land that's untouched in Brazil you can afford to spread out. But there is no one about.

'Er, where is everybody?'

'Well sir, only the government officials can live in Brasilia; all the other people who do the work with the hands and the shops and the cleaning and all these things, they have to live outside in the satellite towns. I will now give you a satellite town.'

And he gives us a satellite town about six miles outside Brasilia. It's simply an enormous collection of little huts, little breeze block huts gathered together in rows. It is *terrible*.

'You have to be very lucky to get allocated one of these houses, sir.'

'Oh, and where do those live who are not allocated houses?'

'I will give you that now sir.'

And he gives it to us: a gigantic wooden slum seven miles outside the capital. You can see the shining towers of the promised city from the top of any of the heaps of garbage that pucker up like scabs on the trodden earth streets. It's another of the brilliant do-it-yourself favellas that the Brazilians are so good at. A vast ramshackle city of wooden shacks built of old packing cases. It crawls all over the countryside, hopelessly out of control, each little shack holding up the next one. And as we stand talking in the hot sunshine, in that disgusting, tumbledown, tea-chest metropolis I can't help noticing how very picturesque the place is. It's throbbing with energy and bursting with colour. Thousands of men, women, children, dogs, chickens are scratching, tumbling, strutting, laughing, talking, eating, arguing, fighting, playing all over the place. A quarter of a million of them live here in bright shirts and gay dresses or in drab rags and sacks with, in the distance, their forbidden city. Their glorious capital. Built regardless of expense. What can they think about it? There it stands, in the sunlight, an aloof lump of cold conceit. It has been built by the administrators for themselves as a fine theoretical conception of the lovely life, while the people whom the administrators are supposed to administer live the life as it really is—a rough and tumble skirmish in the dirt.

You cannot possibly visit Brasilia without having your senses jolted, tickled and kicked around and so it's quite a relief to get back to Rio. When you think of the millions and millions that were hurled away so that the Brazilian Government could have Brasilia! There is absolutely no justification at all in spending money on an article simply because you want it—*waawaawaawaa* . . .

'Good afternoon, gentlemen. Did you have a good trip?'

'Eh? Oh, yes.'

Here we are back in the lizard's shop again. There he is with his lizard face, with glasses on and a trilby hat. 'You had a good trip? What would you like to see today? The amethysts?' He brings out his soft leather pouch and shoots the amethysts over the black velvet. The amethysts, the amethysts, the amethysts! I must have one! I *must* have one! No, I'll have five or six. I'll keep two and give the others away. Yes, they'll make very nice presents.

Well, if you are lucky enough to be able to travel around the world the least you can do, the very least you can do, is to take back some presents for those who had to stay at home.

CHAPTER SIX

Rotting in Paradise

It's happened before of course. It'll happen again no doubt.
I've no idea where I am. The ceiling tells me nothing. A
blank sheet of paper, grey paper. It's not quite light yet. Or
quite dark? Which is it? Well, when you choose to move
around from country to country, from hotel to hotel, it often
happens that when you wake in the morning you don't know
where you are. You're in a bed, yes, there's a wardrobe
staring at you, waiting for you to get up and drag that pair of
trousers from its inside. It's a very fed-up looking wardrobe.
Hotel wardrobes usually are. Well, the stuff that gets bunged
in them. Stuff smelling of mothballs, peppermint, perfume
and cigars to mention but a few. Oh yes, you come across
some well-polluted wardrobes when you travel around. But
although you don't know where you are when you first roll
back your eyelids, you soon do. That incredible little
mini-computer that we get rent-free comes up with the
answer in a couple of seconds and flashes the green light:
don't worry, you are quite safe. You know where you are
now, *yes*, you're in Tahiti!

The first thing that they do to you when you arrive at
Tahiti is to fumigate your luggage. Yes, they fumigate your
luggage. Tubby Foster is a bit put-out by this and so am I.

'That's not very nice, is it?' Tubby says.

'No—carries a nasty stigma, fumigation, you know.' Two
things my mother always dreaded: one was being knocked
down and taken to hospital in dirty underwear, the other was
the authorities arriving with an order to fumigate the house.
That was the most terrible slur that could be visited on a

71

household. Neither of these things ever happened, thank goodness, but the dread of fumigation has been handed down to me quite naturally.

'It's a blinking sauce, isn't it Tubby, fumigating our luggage?'

'Yes, you shouldn't have got off the aeroplane scratching like that—sure to cause trouble.'

'I wasn't scratching much!'

'You were!' accused Tubby. 'Look at you—your arms look as though you've got chicken pox!'

'Everybody knows they're mosquito bites!'

'Ah well, can't be too careful you know.'

They're being jolly careful, if you ask me, they've had our luggage now nearly an hour and they put it in ovens (so they say) and give it a good old chemical baking.

'You've never had anything nasty have you, Johnny, you know—something they might have found out about like nits in the hair, you were scratching your head just now.'

That's another mosquito bite although I feel as though I've got nits or something. But they're not after nits or sheep tick or scabies or lice or fleas or bugs or . . . I won't go on. They are after, believe it or not, rhinoceros beetles.

'Rhinoceros beetles! You haven't picked any up, have you, and not said anything about it? Come on, you might as well own up now, you don't want to be caught with all those rhinoceros beetles in your underwear, do you? When did you first start picking up rhinoceros beetles like this and concealing them in your pants?' Tubby exclaims. A rhinoceros beetle is as big as a walnut with a great big turned-up nose.

It's rather funny when you come to think about it. I can hardly believe that they are really serious about the rhinoceros beetle—by jingo, you'd know if you had one, it could practically charge you and knock you down.

'Perhaps it's the larvae of the rhinoceros beetle that they are nervous about,' suggests Tubby.

Could be, and of course they have very good reason to be nervous of the rhinoceros beetle, for it is death to the coconut palm. Rhinoceros beetles and stick insects simply eat

72

coconut palms. They can turn a beautiful, feathery, verdant palm into just a stupid bald pole sticking up with nothing to do. We have seen acres of such poles on some islands in the Pacific, where once grew thumping coconuts. And on Tahiti they have yet another coconut demolisher. Pretty well every palm tree has nailed around its middle a silvery band of slippery tin, a band of tin about eighteen inches wide to stop the rats from scrabbling up after the coconuts.

The plagues that have descended on Tahiti! Rhinoceros beetles, stick insects, rats and now us. The tourist, the holiday-maker, the side-tripper, the stop-offer, the taker-inner, now all come to Tahiti. The great white hotels are growing on the beaches, the swimming pools glitter right beside the glittering lagoon, the speedboats buzz the bay all day long towing the manly and the beautiful. The skin-divers, the snorkellers, the beach-ballers, and boozers all fill in the blue sunny days just as the pamphlet suggests.

This is the land of the pamphlet holiday. The whole of the South Pacific is being turned into a lounging ground of the pamphlet holiday. And it's a perfect-looking pamphlet if you like that sort of thing. Glossy paper, coloured pictures, the luxury hotel, the dining room with the tables laid and the waiters waiting, the beach bar with the bamboo stools, the seductive bedrooms with twin beds and phone, the blue-green pool all bosomed and bottomed, the laughing, the singing, the dancing at night . . . this is the pamphlet holiday. And it's the same wherever you go. Like airports the world over, pamphlet holidays are the same. Doesn't matter really where you are, you needn't go all the way to Tahiti for a pamphlet holiday, because the holiday and the pamphlet read the same wherever you are. 'Enjoy the thrill of water-skiing or relax in comfort by a crystal-clear pool, or if you prefer, stroll through the tropical gardens or have an ice-cool drink in the beach bar. Breakfast on exotic tropical fruits, dance to native music at night . . .'

Now I don't know whether the pamphlets influence the people or the people influence the pamphlets, but you can't help noticing the way a pamphlet comes to life with real people all acting their pamphlet parts. Everywhere you look people are enjoying this or preferring that or relaxing here or thrilling there. Except those two at breakfast are not fitting into the pamphlet world today. They've had a bit of a tiff in the luxurious bedroom and are not speaking. They should be smiling over their exotic grapefruit, but they're scowling over their runny egg. He goes off to enjoy the thrill of water-skiing, she prefers to sulk in the tropical garden. He enjoys about fifteen ice-cool drinks in the beach bar and gets sloshed, she prefers to relax by the crystal-clear pool. But it's much too hot in the sun and she miserably swims a few lengths. They dance at night with different partners, and both look very unpamphlet-like. This will never do, so why not enjoy the thrill of a kiss and make up, or if you prefer take the first plane out in the morning?

Mind you, the pamphlet holiday on Tahiti is pretty good. We enjoyed the thrill of sailing and preferred to relax by the pool quite a bit, and scarcely passed the beach bar without dropping in. But although it's fine for us there are many of the natives of these islands who do not like the way things have changed in the last few years. They do not like the strangers who come to their beautiful island jangling dollars, dangling cameras, jingling bags, gangling and haggling. They do not like the strangers who demand attention and service, and clean linen, and iced water, and breakfast and lunch and dinner, and facilities to cash cheques, and send cables and forward mail, and order flowers and call cabs. They turn every day into an irritable whirlwind of triviality in a land once tranquil and calm. It is understandable that they do not really want this—after all life was perfectly agreeable before all this happened. Now every day is one blessed whirlwind after another, since the jets started to fly in and the great white hotels grew on the beach and they came with the glass-bottomed boats and aqualungs and speedboats and water skis.

And now they come in to stop overnight! Now that is real hell! Imagine 120 senior citizens on a world jet air tour, arriving in a paradise of white sand, blue sky, a champagne sea, hibiscus flowers, bougainvillea and coconut palms. They are all wearing leis. Yes, *leis*. It is the custom in these parts when you arrive at an island you are given a sort of daisy chain of frangipani to wear around your neck. A lei. Now most of the people who make these world tours are senior citizens, because junior citizens do not have the money to make these sort of trips. And worthy though senior citizens may be they do present an astonishing picture in their South Sea island gear with leis around their dear old stooping necks, and leather trappings hanging from them like battle-worn crusaders. Tons of luggage tumbles all around them, and the hallway of the hotel looks like the aftermath of the battle scene from *Gone with the Wind*.

Mind you, they have travelled with considerable bravery for it is a very brave thing to do—biff around the world by jet late in life. And they have stood up to it very well indeed, but the strain is beginning to show here and there. Well, when 120 people arrive at one hotel all at once they have got to be booked in. And booking in takes time. So they have to line up to be booked in. There is no other way. Three lines of them, and every person in every line with his or her own personal problem.

'Yes, well, we don't want to have to be at the back of the block.'

'No sir. Your name, please sir?'

'Bergmuller.'

'Mr Bergmuller, you and Mrs Bergmuller—right?—you have room 420. It does not face the sea, but it is a very nice room.'

'Why do we always have to be at the back of the block?'

'Well sir, it is very difficult. Perhaps you can arrange something with somebody in your group eh?'

'Yeah, okay, okay. Do you have any mail for me?'

'Could you enquire at the end, sir?'

'Oh, can't you?'

'No, sir, I am to do with the reservations. Could I see your passports, please?'

'Passports?'

'Yes, sir. They will be returned to you in the morning.'

'Well, well . . . I don't have my—er—my—er—my wife—er—she has them, I guess.'

'Yes sir, but I need your passports.'

'Oh gee, er Claire? Claire?' But Claire has ambled off into the gift shop and is staring at a tray of South Sea island sea shells. 'Claire! Claire!'

Oh, you need to be fit to travel this way. You mustn't get ill. I did, and it was all very frightening. I got malaria. Well, it seemed like it. Late in the afternoon I felt hot, very hot. I had a temperature, quite a high temperature. I thought of all those mosquito bites I had collected. If the authorities find out that I've got malaria they'll come around and fumigate me, I thought, and I couldn't stand that. I'll keep quiet about it. Not a word. I lay on the bed staring at that blank ceiling, calculating that my temperature must be about 104 degrees. 'You coming down to dinner?' Tubby asked.

'You know, I don't think I will tonight.'

'What's the matter? Not feeling too good?'

'So-so.'

'Touch of the sun perhaps?'

'Could be.'

'Shall I call a doctor?'

'Oh no.'

'Sure?'

'Yes I'll be all right in the morning.'

But I'm not all right in the morning—but I haven't got malaria. It's *worse* than that. I'm going rotten! Oh, there's no doubt about it. I am going rotten, just going physically rotten. Mind you, I've got it all covered up with sticking plaster, but it's rotten underneath. I don't think it's leprosy yet. But whatever it is, it's catching up with the unrotten bits of me very fast. It started with the mosquito bites on my feet and then on my arms. I know I'd been scratching them, but you've got to give them a bit of a bash now and again, and they started to go *rotten*. I'll skip the similes and the metaphors for all our sakes, but if you can just keep a rotting pear and a custard tart somewhere in your mind's eye you will realise the sort of rotten state I am in. I've always had a mild interest in chemistry and gardening, and to me it's morbidly interesting to find that I am behaving like a compost heap. In the same way that a compost heap generates a dramatic smouldering heat as it rots I too, as I rot, am generating enough heat to fry an egg or boil a kettle or any similar stunt that the *Guinness Book of Records* might find interesting.

But I suffer in silence as we walk the streets of Papeete, the principal town of Tahiti. It must be said of Tahiti that it is a most beautiful island, a volcanic island that has covered itself with rich vegetation and glorious, wonderful flowers. It squats in the blue Pacific, a great jagged hump of green. Only a narrow strip around the coast is of any use for cultivation or development—the interior is mountainous and impassable and useless for agriculture. It's like a great green bowler hat with people living in the brim. A handsome, good-looking people. A truly striking lot of people, especially of course the women. They have taken from the French that slick dash of style, the style that is aloof, unapproachable, most provocative and supremely confident. Oh they really are something! With even brown skin, long black hair decorated with flowers, wearing flowery mini dresses all a size too small, they challenge every man without so much as glancing at him. They are the girls that Gauguin painted, no longer naked and innocent or frightened of ghosts. They are nicely dished up, they know exactly what life is about and are not a bit fearful of this life, the next or the last. They cruise around in cars, skid about on scooters, buzz about on bikes, and they all of them know exactly what effect they are having on those who like that sort of thing.

Oh yes, a stroll around Papeete makes very pleasant viewing and the port of Papeete itself is a very pleasant place. It is in fact a shanty town. A good-class shanty town, but a shanty town. It's true some of the big banks are pushing their great slab stone buildings in here and there the way that bullying big banks do, but Papeete is largely a shanty town. But a very well-ordered shanty town with pretty wooden shops and houses, covered walks, wooden verandahs, balconies and white wooden churches, holy and clean. The streets are narrow, they smell of fish and the sea and spice. And right behind the town the rich green mountain rushes up almost vertically into a boiling steam white cloud.

Oh yes, Papeete is a town of the dear, dead past. But of course its days are numbered. A sweeping two-lane highway already runs right along the front, the concrete lampposts are up and it's plain to see that one bulldozer could shove the whole of Papeete on to the bonfire in one afternoon. It may have happened by now. But that's how I remember it through the haze of my own compost heap central heating.

It was strange: walking about this shanty town I gradually became a sort of shanty town character. Well, my rotten left foot simply could not stand the chafing of the sandal strap upon it any more. The sticking plaster was no longer holding but flapping about. I was walking with a most dramatic limp. ff*bump* ff*bump* fff*bump*. A Chinese shop-keeper gives me a slit-eyed look as I lope past his heap of melons, ffff*bump*; two little Tahitian girls skipping in an alley stop and gawp as I lurch by, fff*bump* fff*bump*, they stare with fear and fascination, fff*bump* fff*bump*; a mangy mongrel cur drags his ribs out of my way, his eyes pleading (he has reason to believe that I went lame kicking dogs to death) fff*bump*.

'Is your foot playing you up a bit?'

'Just a bit.'

'It would be a good idea to pop in and see a doctor.'

'No no no, goodness knows what they would do to you out here! It's getting better actually, I think, fff*bump*—Now why didn't I think of that before? Of course! How to cure the halt and the lame in a few seconds. Well, at least half the people of these islands walk about with nothing on their feet.

'It's the sandals that are killing you, take them off!' It's quite normal to walk about with bare feet. That's better. *Ah* yes, it's much better. The pavements are a bit hot though but I can stand that all right. The knack is to walk in the shade as much as possible, and walk on the ball of the foot in the hot spots.

'Crumbs, they are hot, these pavements!'

'Where're your sandals?'

'I've taken them off.'

'You can't walk about like that! Come on, come and see a doctor.'

'Look, I've worked it out. If I buy a pair of rubber

plimsolls, a pair of daps, and cut the toecaps out then my foot won't get chafed!'

'You're off your loaf! You know that, don't you? If you don't get that foot attended to it'll *drop off* or something.'

'Don't talk so daft!'

But strange things happen to the mind when it's got a compost heap steaming underneath it . . . I remember I went into a chemist's—not to buy ointment or soothing balm or disinfectant, but to buy a packet of razor blades. Yes, a packet of razor blades—you see how devious and cunning is the deranged mind when it has really made up its mind to go its own mad way. I bought a packet of razor blades to cut the toecaps out of the daps that I had not yet bought. I remember walking into the shoe shop to buy the daps.

'Look, this isn't going to do any good.' Tubby tried to dissuade me.

'Oh *do* be quiet.'

There are three girl assistants packing shoes or something with tissue paper. They are using lots of tissue paper. I remember how it rustled as they scampered through it to get to the other side of the shop away from me, like the sound of a lot of swans taking off from a small pond surrounded by trees. And there they cringed, behind the counter as far away from us as they could get. Well, being shoe shop assistants the first thing they look at, on any customer entering their shop, is the feet. They got the measure of my feet in about a second and a half and they bolted, the three of them, it was perfectly clear that they were not coming near me. And I was highly indignant and incensed. Gentle listener, should you meet a madman let him go about his business his own sweet mad way. Unless he looks like doing himself or others an injury thwart him not, for he is mad, the logic of this life has left him he sees things that you do not see, you see things to which he is blind. He alone knows what he wants to do. *Let him do it.* If you don't he is dynamite.

'Look, you don't want any daps.'

'I *do* want the daps, I've got the razor blades, haven't I? Of course I want some daps, not much to ask is it, a pair of daps? What's the matter with everybody?' You will notice that madmen always ask what is the matter with everybody else. The madder a person the more sure is he of his own sanity. 'I need some daps, I've got the razor blades!' What sort of sense does that make? Rather dangerous sense as far as the razor blades are concerned.

The three girls huddle together trying to look as though nothing is the matter. And I honestly cannot understand why I am being refused attention in this shoe shop. I can't understand it. There I stand in the middle of a rather smart sort of shoe shop, on rather a choice pale blue carpet with bare feet. One foot is plainly out of condition and going rotten, and they are both smeared in tar and shanty-town filth and grit, and I expect to try on shoes—not only try them on, but I also expect those girls to help me with shoe horns and things. And they do nothing about me, they whisper darkly and never look my way. And I need daps very badly, very badly indeed. I *need* daps, I've got the razor blades. All right, I'll get my own daps! And I help myself to daps. I hobble about the shop in a fury opening boxes, scattering tissue paper, rattling cardboard. I know what I want all right and I'll find it! There, that's it! Just the thing, daps.

I take the daps in their box and go over to the girls. 'It's all right, it's all right, I'll pay. Blinking place this is, it's a wonder that you manage to sell a blinking shoe all blinking day long! I'm never coming in here again, that's a fact!'

I snatch the change and with the daps in their box and the razor blades in my pocket I stomp out of the shop barefoot, and I'm astonished to hear Tubby Foster say, 'Thank you very much, good morning, thank you.'

'Why do you thank them? They did nothing, absolutely nothing! Thank them, my foot!'

'Yes well, you know.'

'I *don't* know.'

'Sorry.'

You know, you can measure a friendship by the amount of madness your friends are prepared to endure from you. Tubby Foster was a friend indeed. He hung around as I went about my madness in case I got into serious trouble. Mind you, he was fascinated as well I think, because he didn't know that I was suffering a raging temperature. He thought that I was going off my chump. Well, there I was sitting on the kerb cutting the toecaps out of the daps with a razor blade.

'They look a bit funny, don't they?' tried Tubby.

'They don't.'

'Sorry.'

The daps look like old boots that tramps wear in the comics. Still, I've done what I meant to do. I'll soon be able to walk about, you'll see. Now one of the fortunate things about madness is that it is very exhausting. You go absolutely flat-out with twice the energy and purpose of a normal person, and then you collapse. I collapsed when I tried to put the daps on. They were at least two sizes too small. I had sold myself a pair of daps, cut the toecaps out of them with a razor blade, and I couldn't even get them on my poor, aching, rotten feet. Oh dear, oh dear what shall I do?

'You can't take them back to the shop.'

'I know.'

'The doctor is just here, come on!'

And Tubby Foster led me like a well-trained spaniel into the doctor's. The doctor is a tall efficient Frenchman.

'Ah, what have we 'ere, eh?'

'I don't know.'

'You are leaving it a long time, eh?'

'Mmm.'

'You are feeling 'ot, eh?'

'I'm on fire, I think.'

'Yeah. You know what you have?'

'No.'

'It is quite common, you know. We call it staf—you have heard of staf?'

'Staf?'

'Yeah, it is a staphylococcus infection—staf.'

'Is it serious?'

'Poof! Look at it—it spreads very quick, eh?'

'Oh.'

'But it is easy to put right, you know. A few days and it will be gone!'

81

It's quite incredible how a simple reassurance will turn madness to sanity. 'Oh good, well what do we do?' It is very simple: antibiotics and some good clean dressings. He cleaned my foot, and bound it up in no time at all, and when I came out Tubby Foster was in the waiting room with my sandals.

'Do you want your sandals?'

'Oh, thanks.'

Sandals. I put them on, I've been obsessed with daps. But I can wear the sandals now and they're quite comfortable and as we break into the sunshine from the doctor's surgery there are the daps in the gutter where I had left them.

'Taking your daps with you?'

'Give over, I must have been mad!' Yes, but better now. I need to be, for there lie the daps pigeon-toed in the gutter, new daps mutilated almost beyond recognition. And there we leave them.

'What do you want to do?'

'Just go and lie down and look at that ceiling in the hotel bedroom.'

I know it's not very comforting but at least I'll know where I am. And I do need to know that.

CHAPTER SEVEN

A Tequila Picnic

It rains every day in Mexico City around about tea time. Well, that is what has happened every day since we have been here and according to the reception desk clerk at the Hotel Campana the weather is running pretty true to form.

'Si, señor, at this time of the year every day perhaps a little rain, perhaps plenty rain in the afternoon, si si si.' A great white smile cracks his face open, 'Si si si, every day little rain, plenty rain, si si.'

He likes his climate, he wants me to like his climate. And you can't help liking it. It would suit most people down to the ground, knocking off at quarter past four because of rain every day. But rain every day is nothing like as miserable as it sounds, oh no, because for most of the day the weather is fresh and lively. Mexico City is called the city of perpetual spring. And a good perpetual spring takes a lot of beating. Why is this city so blessed? Well, if you look at the map (and if you don't it doesn't matter because it's all as clear as the spring air) you will see that Mexico City is very near the equator. That's hot, that's bad. Ah yes, but it spreads itself out at an altitude of over 7,000 feet, which keeps it cool. Not only that, it lies at the bottom of an enormous saucer—the rim of that saucer being a great circle of mountains. So you see, being in the bottom of a saucer, very close to the equator, in the sun *and* high up in cooler air you have all the opposing physical forces nicely lined up to pull and push, mingle and mix, thunder and flash and rumble and rain.

And at this time of the year, August, that is what happens. More often than not the day starts blue, bright and shining.

83

From the restaurant on the sixth floor of the Hotel Campana you can see right away to the mountains beyond the city. There's that lovely old volcano Popocatepetl, the warrior, still wearing his old white night-cap of snow. He's been asleep now for years and years. He'll never wake again, they say.

But the city is more than awake. A thousand coloured taxi-cabs go screaming around the great square down below. Now the only way to get around Mexico City is by taxi. There are trams and buses of course. Indeed, there are two classes of buses but goodness knows where they go and when they go. And so you've got to use taxis. The taxis of Mexico City are probably the most unique in the world. They are painted with bright bobby-dazzler paints. The average Mexican taxi looks like the advance publicity vehicle of some brokendown and tatty circus, and all the drivers look like sword swallowers, fire eaters or tightrope walkers and quite a few look as though they are often fired from cannons. But say what you will about how they look, they all have a wonderful reckless circus air about them and they all drive as though they were taking part in the grand finale chariot race.

Until you get used to this, and it can take a long time, I estimate that you can have a whole year knocked off your alloted span every time you travel by taxi. Well, some of these taxis you wouldn't give a fiver for. They are clapped out old bangers, battletrap wrecks. Any British Ministry of Transport vehicle inspector would have a convulsion if he saw one of these boneshakers. Or would he? That's the surprising thing about them—they all seem to work. They can all stop in time . . . *just*. And that's all that matters. As long as you can stop—and you'll stop all right—you won't come to any harm. Well, how can you come to harm if you have a statue of the madonna screwed on the ledge above the bashed-up dashboard? She'll rattle quite a bit mind you (well, the screw that holds her there has been put on cross-threaded and that's as tight as she'll go). Still, she'll see that you are all right, especially if you put a few flowers in the chromium ice-cream cone tied to the taxi-meter.

They are homely little hovels inside some of these cabs,

and the circus drivers are just about as lively and chatty a
tribe of nomads as you could find anywhere. They know at
once, of course, that we are foreigners and that makes a bit of
a change for them.

Ah buenas dias, señor.'

'Buenas dias.'

'Americano, si?'

'Americano, tut.' I give him the official Spanish no, the
forefinger wagging like a windscreen wiper and a 'tut'.
'Americano tut.' It is the most definite no. It's absolutely
final—the finger wag and the 'tut'.

'No Americano?'

'Tut.'

'Allemagna si?'

'No Allemagna. Allemagna tut. Ingles.'

'Ah, Ingles! Manchester Ooneeted? Mancheester Oooneeted?'

'Manchester United, si si.'

'Manchester Oooneeted. Winson Shurshill.'

'Winston Churchill, si si.'

'Bobbee Sharleton.'

'Bobby Charlton, si si, Winston Churchill.'

'Winson Shurshill, Mancheester Oooneeted, Bobby
Sharlton, si si ahahahahah.'

He's so happy! What a lovely picture of England he
has—Winston Churchill, Bobby Charlton, Manchester
United. I'll never forget him, he was so keen to get his
pronunciation right and I was trying to help him with
Manchester United.

'Look, Manchester United.'

'Mansheester Oooonited?'

'No, United.'

'Ooooo . . .'

'Uuuuuu . . .' I was sitting beside him, he was watching
my lips carefully. 'Uuuuu . . .'

'Ooooo . . .'

'Uuuuu . . .'

'Oooo . . .'

We were rattling down this great avenue, he wasn't

85

looking where he was going at all, he was looking at my lips ('Uuuuu,' 'Ooooo') when suddenly he slapped on his brakes and we stopped with a dreadful judder four inches away from a stationary tramcar. He did this looking straight at me, he never looked towards the tramcar once. How did he know it was there? Well, it must have been the madonna of the dashboard. She'd saved him again. Mind you, she was brought up with a bit of a jolt on her loose screw, and she was shaking her head at him like a goalkeeper who has been sadly let down by his fullbacks. She's saying, ''Ere, watchit Alfonso! I can't bring off those sort of saves every five minutes you know. Can't expect miracles, can you eh?'

But that was a miracle. They happen to all the taxis, all the time, all over Mexico City. And after a while you cease to sit in your seat in frozen terror and a strange calm settles on you when you realise that all you need is faith. If you have faith you will be saved. And when you look at some of the Mexican taxis that's about all there is to save you—faith.

There are different classes of taxis in Mexico City: there are cabs that ply for hire anywhere, there are cabs that you call from a cab stand, there are cabs that you can hire by the hour and there are cabs that only operate over certain specified routes. And they are very, very cheap. They are called pesero cabs and I think we could learn a thing or two from this system. They are in fact taxis that behave like little buses. They have certain limits, and run up and down main roads, say from Shepherd's Bush to St Paul's and back. Like buses they do not deviate from that route, they pick up and drop passengers all along the line and there is just one rate. Twenty years ago it was just sixpence—dirt cheap. You can always tell when a pesero cab driver has room in his cab—he drives along with his arm held high out of the side window with one finger pointing to the sky: room for one more.

Of course the pesero cabs are very cheap and very efficient, but I was never able to find out exactly how many passengers any one cab was supposed to carry. Well, it can be embarrassing for an Englishman to be suddenly packed into a tiny box with half a dozen totally strange, dark and curly Mexicans. I mean, you feel that you ought to introduce yourself or something. They're all very nice and charming, but, naturally there's no point in trying to start a conversation because everyone will be getting out in a minute. And so we jog along, hunched up in a sweaty scrum each with his own private thoughts. Every now and again you find a pair of calculating brown eyes levelled at you, wondering. You gaze back and the eyes swivel away, and quiver at the palm trees waving past the windows. And still the driver drives on with one finger pointing to the blue sky: room for one more. Room for one more? It's impossible! I mean, we are all sitting sideways as it is to make as much room as possible.

Room for one more! Oh and here is one more, standing at the pavement's edge waving to the cab to stop: a lady. One of those fascinating ladies who look as though they've just been turned out of a beautiful jelly mould. Round and controlled. Wonderfully inflated with all the correct tyre pressures everywhere—28 front 26 back. To say that she was a dish would be doing her a big injustice. She is a lord mayor's banquet. The dark brown eyes inside the cab begin to swish and flash, the moustaches tremble, the nostrils twitch, as this monumental well-set jelly gracefully squeezes and squeaks itself into the cab. We all squirm and shove and compress and the best we can do is to leave about seven inches of cab seat all for her very own. The cab was a bit quick off the mark of course, and she wallowed back into the corner with a well-padded thud overlapping on to me.

I don't think that I have ever been placed so suddenly in such close proximity with a total stranger in my life. We have to lie sideways, jammed together and looking into each other's faces. We might for all the world be in bed together. What do you say? You've got to say something. What's the Spanish for 'Sorry about all this, don't mind me?' But I can't say a word. Worse still, my arms are jammed between us and this is very awkward. I try to pull one arm from out of this billowing muddle to make more room. She flashes me a hot Mexican glance that translates into English quickly as: 'Ere, that'll do! Sorry, I was trying to get my arm out, you know, make things a bit more, you know. It's no good—there is

87

nothing you can say even if you could say it.

And so lying partly-submerged by this beautiful jelly we clatter along, our eyes meeting with a bang halfway across the five-inch gulf that separates them. Still, the great thing about the pesero taxi-cab is that it's cheap and handy, and you are quite prepared to put up with a bit of discomfort to save a bob or two.

We get out at Chapultepec Park. Chapultepec Park is a tremendous open park; several grand avenues run through it. The blazing bobby-dazzler taxis rattle in and out of the trees, the rich self-satisfied limousines squelch through the high, waving palm trees and the whole glorious rough and tumble of the highways, byways, back streets and alleys spreads itself all over the dark green grass of Chapultepec Park.

It's an incredible sight because everybody brings their lunch with them. So, splattered about amongst the hibiscus, the oleanders, the bougainvillea and the palm trees are random dabs of happy families, sprawling about on their day of rest and eating and drinking and squawking and shrieking. Now a Mexican picnic is not the sort of picnic we are used to at all. It's not a neat packet of cheese and tomato sandwiches, a convenient vacuum flask of coffee and a well chosen Williams pear and a fruit knife. No, when a Mexican goes on a picnic, Santa Maria, he goes on a picnic! I mean, if you're going to have a Sunday lunch out you're going to have Sunday lunch out. And so the Mexican takes on his picnic his whole family and everything that he's got in his kitchen. Yes, that includes the kitchen stove.

And you get to Chapultepec Park nice and early, so that you get that gentle sloping pitch just under the trees near the lake. That slope is just right for snoozing on, you see, if you don't fancy your hammock—but first of all let's get the grub out!

Now Mexican food is a law unto itself. Before sampling Mexican food you should equip yourself with a bomb detector, because quite a lot of Mexican food explodes in your mouth. And you can never be quite sure which is the explosive sort. It could be that pale green, innocent-looking mash that resembles a Russian salad someone has trodden in. That explodes. I know, I had some once. The first taste has a seven-second delaying device built into it, before it explodes in your mouth and your ears blow off, your eyes roll over backwards, and your throat constricts and seizes up trying to protect the stomach from getting blown to smithereens. Perhaps you get used to it in time. I never did. A sizzling Madras curry hurled together by a heavy-handed cook is but a vanilla ice-cream compared to some Mexican explosive devices. Fantastico.

Just look what that family of fifteen has spread about all over the grass for itself. It's a proper firework display of explosive food. Flaming red dishes of molten volcanic lava—Mount Etna in eruption; seething green glowing bowls of Merlin the magician; spinning platters of multi-coloured Catherine wheels; brown pots of squibs; tins of Jackie Jumpers; packets of sparklers and bottles of rockets. It's an incredible set piece.

And they are getting stuck into it. No knives or forks of course, certainly not. You use the all purpose, easy-to-make-and-carry tortilla. The tortilla forms the basis of many Mexican diets. It is roughly a thin, leathery pancake, and is usually lobbed up about the size of an extended-play 45 record. A Mexican housewife makes tortillas every day. It is the daily bread, except that it is not made with wheat, it is made with flour ground out of corn (Indian corn, sweet corn, maize, corn on the cob—call it what you like; all those names mean roughly the same thing) and it is from this and a little water that the tortilla is made, by griddling it on a hot dry griddle. No fat of any sort is used.

Now I have said that the tortilla is rather leathery. This is not a criticism because it was designed that way. A tortilla is not only a thing that you eat; it is also a thing that you use and so it has to be durable. You *could* use it, of course, for lots of things like patching sofas or barrage balloons, or it would make a very good mustard plaster or a kettle holder, or you could re-seat a shooting stick with it or slip it inside a loosely fitting shoe or wear it like an informal beret. The tortilla is really something that no one should be without, when you come to think of it. But the generally accepted way of using a tortilla is to roll it up in the form of a tube, then you can scoop this tube into the assorted firework dishes and you're off! The tortilla is an eating tool—and you eat it as you use it. When you've eaten through one item of leathery cutlery you take another one.

That roistering family of fifteen are really going it, passing around the popping, banging bowls, the tortillas plunging in and out, sizzling and crackling. This is great and glorious powerful grub. This is the place to eat it: Chapultepec Park. You can behave as you like here. Nobody cares. Nobody says No. Sunday is a day of Yes. The rest of the week is No. Sunday is Yes. Yes, you can do what you like. Yes, you can lie about. Yes, you can walk all over the grass. Yes, you can drink what you like when you like. That old man there, he must be the grandfather of the family of fifteen. He's spotted us watching them and he's coming over to us with a bottle in his hand. He looks to be the most awful, bloodthirsty brigand that ever slit a throat. But smile at him and his face splits in two with the most delightful grin.

'Ah, señor!' He pushes the bottle into my hands and puts a withered brown hand on my shoulder and looks hard into my eyes. He really is a dirty old man, but a delightfully dirty old man. He smells and looks like a brown chopping board, a board that has had everything chopped on it for years: garlic, onions, cabbage, carrots, sage, onions, garlic, fish, meat, sausage, onions, celery, turnips, garlic, chives, rhubarb, onions, cheese, garlic, pimentos, apples, onions . . . He is a sort of living, walking, breathing, bouquet garni. Especially when he smiles. He's *beautiful*. 'Ah, señor Amigo!' Phew, what a wonderful smell!

'Gracias, señor, what is in the bottle eh?' I ask. He makes the Spanish national gesture for drinking—the fingers clenched, the thumb stuck out pointing down the open mouth towards the throat.

'Well, what do you think? He seems to be doing all right on it.'

'Oh yes.' Tubby agrees. 'Probably do you a lot of good.'

I take a gentle swig at the bottle. *Oooo*, that's it all right. Tequila.

'Tequila, si?'

'Si, tequila. Bueno si?'

'Si bueno.'

The chopping board forces the bottle of tequila on Tubby Foster and then back to me again. 'No, no gracias, no no.'

'Si si si, mas mas (more more).'

'No no.' Well you've got to be careful with this tequila. It's a spirit distilled from the juice of cactus, and with that promising and prickly beginning tequila sets off through life with the avowed intention of slaughtering all who are free and easy with it. You must not muck about with too much tequila so: 'Thanks very much, no more, no gracias.'

'Si, *mas, mas*.' The chopping board suddenly turns very fierce. He holds the bottle underneath my nose. '*Mas, mas!*'

Oh well, never let it be said. I take a good swig of the five-star high octane and breathe the lethal vapours back at the old chopping board for a change. He loves that. He puts his arm around my shoulder and grins. Amigo, amigo. The deadly bottle is passed around again. Chapultepec Park spins slowly twice. The picnic party under the tree spins with it and so do the 50,000 other picnic parties all banging away with the firework food in Chapultepec Park.

We do manage to get away from the chopping board eventually, mainly because he seemed to be getting rather tired and floppy. His sons and daughters had slung him a hammock between the trees, and he's slumped into it, still hanging on to his empty tequila bottle.

The Mexicans are great hammock slingers. Wherever they have picnics they sling their hammocks and hang their trappings in the trees. They turn the place into a sort of encampment in a couple of minutes and Chapultepec Park on Sunday is a tremendous raggle-taggle, slap-happy encampment. Nobody cares. It's a Yes day. Yes, you can do what you like. Yes, you can sell what you like. This is a great place to sell things. Well, the people are here to enjoy themselves so get something to sell. What? You'll find something. Look at that lady there—she's scraped up a couple of pounds of cashew nuts and heaped them on the pathway. They're for sale. Well, somebody might want them. Next to her another lady has knocked up a couple of dozen rock cakes, after all, you never know. Next to her another lady has stewed up a few home-made sweets—well you can't get them in the shops like that, not home-made—at a quarter the usual price. I mean, they're a real bargain if you like that sort of thing. All over the park the freelance traders are selling, selling, selling: biscuits, nuts, fruit, waffles, pastries, doughnuts, chewing gum, sweets, post-cards, crisps, cakes, sausages, coffee, lemonade.

You are not badgered to buy, but if you want anything, well, you know where to get it. The more successful traders have set themselves up with little stalls. That man is plaiting plastic buckets. He plaits very fast and does quite a swift trade—they're cheap, you see. And there's a whole row of ladies making enormous paper flowers. They'll brighten the kitchen up, won't they?

Another line of ladies under the trees is doing hairdres-sing, yes, in the open, in the park. Oh, it's quite professional in a way and its cheap. I mean, you've got no overheads. Well, it's only logical isn't it? Take our Gloria over there—ever since she was a little girl she's loved doing her mother's hair, combing it, brushing it, everybody always said she should have been a hairdresser. But there it is, she had to go to work in this office and now on Sundays she just comes here with her little trestle table, and you can see the women come for miles to have their hair done by Gloria. She makes a lovely job of it. Under the trees—no electricity of course, you don't need electricity in a climate of perpetual spring. All Gloria's clients sit with their dark hair crimped and twisted around blue plastic rollers, while one of Gloria's friends—Carmen—files their nails and dabs them blood red, and another of Gloria's friends—Kataline—smooths their olive faces with mysterious lotions of guaranteed beauty. The eyebrows are black, and the eyelids are shaded green and blue to allure; the lips smarmed red, round and pouty and all this transformation is slowly brought about under the trees at Chapultepec Park. Dozens of ladies are receiving their secret beauty blessings in broad daylight in the park, with the gay caballeros sauntering by, slipping their loose eyes along the lines of mutilated ladies, trying to trace a sign of real beauty through the grease, the paste, and paint and the comical clownish top knots.

Still, if you can get it done cheaply, why not? I don't suppose for a moment you'd be allowed to open a hairdressing establishment in Hyde Park, but you can in Chapultepec Park on Sunday, because Sunday is a Yes day. Yes, we are going to forget all about the week that's gone by. Yes, we are not going to consider the week to come. Yes, we are going to blinking well enjoy ourselves and yes, you know . . . yes, I think it's going to don't you? Yes, I really think it's going to . . .

The sky above the park has suddenly become a rolling blanket of black cloud. Four strong winds come swirling in from the four corners of the park. The shop blinds begin to panic, the scattered newspapers go around in a flap, the balloon-seller is carried by his giant balloons tottering towards the lake. Everybody runs for cover. The traffic police cocoon themselves in oilskins, the lamps swing and squeak and it starts to rain. It always does about quarter past four in Mexico City at this time of the year. It's a lively rain that lashes a bit and then calms down to a passive spring sprinkle. But one thing about it—you know where you are. Tomorrow will be fine and sunny to start with. You know what to do. You're in the city of perpetual spring. At least you know where you are. You know where you are all right.

CHAPTER EIGHT

In Vino Veritas

'Mid pleasures and palaces, exactly exactly, how very true, there's no place like home. Especially if you've been travelling around for several weeks and more especially if you're feeling a bit off-colour. Well, you know when you go abroad you can pick up some funny complaints. And if you're abroad and start getting those stabs of pain in the stomach you do long for home sweet home.

There is something wrong with Tubby Foster. He's so quiet. He's been silent for some days. Not absolutely silent, but quiet bordering on silent. He was perfectly all right when we were in Honfleur and Trouville and Deauville, but I noticed that he was rather subdued by the time we got to the Mont St Michel.

Now it doesn't matter how many times you've been to the Mont St Michel you can always give it another whirl. It's worth it. No matter what you say the place has a wonderful style about it, hasn't it? Yes. There it stands out in the sea, a tremendous cone of granite; buildings hanging on to it like limpets, the whole thing crowned with a beautifully sculptured Benedictine Abbey. A causeway a mile long connects it to the mainland. It's a most formidable and wonderful fortress, impossible to storm and take with bow and arrow or cannonball, we English tried hard enough in the Hundred Years War.

Hundreds of motor cars and coaches are lined at the end of the causeway, the day trippers are stacking up. Of course you can walk to Mont St Michel when the tide is out, and it does go out—right out of sight, leaving a wet haze of sand

and mud and slurry and shimmering slabs of shining water and mystery. And somewhere beyond the haze the sea has gone into hiding. But it will be back, of course, often in the most terrifying way. The popular saying is that the tides rush in here as fast as a horse can gallop. Now that's pretty fast. Can't confirm it because I've never seen it. But the dangers of being cut off and drowned are very real. There's a wonderful notice carefully fixed and clearly printed in English at the entrance to the Mount. 'It is dangerous to risk you in the bay during the rising tide. This can surprise you at each time. Please call for the tides time.'

'Huh, you see? It's dangerous to risk you in the bay during the rising tide.'

'Yes.'

'This can surprise you at each time.'

'Yes.'

'Funny.'

Tubby usually makes a note of whimsical notices like that, but not today. He just looks across the pale quivering sands like a lost Arab wondering what's happened to his oasis.

I try again: 'Tide will be in soon, perhaps.'

'Perhaps.'

'Well, shall we wander up to the top?'

'If you like.'

You can't visit the Mount without going to the top. Everybody goes to the top. Mind you, it's a pretty vicious climb if you happen to be a bit short in the wind and crystallised in the joints. But you've got a job to keep a good day tripper down. Up they go, struggling and hobbling with sticks, helped by sons and daughters, pausing on the bends to suck as much oxygen as they can from the high blue sky, *sssshhhh*. They mean to get to the top or die, and with some it sounds as if it's a fifty-fifty chance, *shhhhhawww*. Must be a coachload from a very smoky industrial area.

We go up with them through the tiny streets. Streets and streets solid with souvenirs. *Sssshhhaaawww*. Streets and streets of tatty trinketry, *ssshhhhaaw*, might buy something on the way down, can't stop to look now, *sssshhhaaaw*. And on we go, slowly, painfully up the steep stone steps—young

95

husbands carrying perambulators, young wives carrying children, old men carrying poodles, old ladies carrying on, *ssshhhaaa*. But we get to the top, oh yes, we get there all right. And flop down, just flop down on the stone steps, lean back on the stone walls, hang over the stone battlements. This day tripping is hard work, you know.

But they soon come back fighting, demanding more. Especially the old ladies. Their energy is quite remarkable, *letendra*. The French language spoken without teeth sounds like someone playing with a garden hose, *letendrai*, or a badly-tuned radio, *letendramen*.

And the orderly mob of sightseers move off to see around the Abbey.

'Shall we go in?'

'No, I'd rather stay in the sun I think.'

What *is* the matter with him? Mmmm, strange. Well perhaps a Cornucopia of Fruits de Mer will bring him back to normal, and a loving bottle of red wine. Oh, we always drink red wine. There is some very nice white wine about I know, but one thing that Tubby and I agree upon is that you can drink red wine with anything. Yes, even shellfish. Well, Fruits de Mer generally speaking does not sport many oysters—it's usually mussels, cockles, whelks, winkles, shrimps and crabs. Fine with a light red wine. Oysters on their own, I grant you, cannot be themselves without a dry white wine.

Now just down there hard by the sea wall is a whole row of very promising looking restaurants.

'Those restaurants look good, don't they?'

'I don't think I want anything to eat.'

'You don't want anything to eat?!'

'No.'

'Why not try an omelette, they make very special omelettes here. You whip up the white of an egg into a stiff froth and fold the yolks into it, so that you get an omelette like a sponge cake. Well, it's an experience anyway.'

'Oh all right, let's try that and a bottle of red wine.'

'Unlike you to have just an omelette.'

'Yes.'

'Huh—anything wrong?'

'Yes.'

Well, thank goodness for that. I knew there was something wrong but now that I'm about to know I can't help thinking that I may be the cause of the wrong. Something I said, something I did? Perhaps I've forgotten that I borrowed 100 francs and didn't pay it back again. But I *did* pay it back. What can it be? I never expected the answer I got—who would expect an answer so bizarre, surrealist, so barmy and Dali-like?

'Well, what is the matter?'

'I've got a black tongue.'

'I beg your pardon?'

'I've got a black tongue.'

'Hahahahaha, get out, what, you've got a black tongue? No!'

'You've asked me, I've told you. I've got a black tongue.'

He means it! 'How black?' It was a daft question—how black. Black's black, and to emphasise the point Tubby just stuck his tongue out at me, leaving it out for a second and withdrawing it back in a flash. Good heavens! It *was* black!

'It's absolutely black.'

'I know it is, I *told* you it was.'

'I know, I know, I'm sorry . . . gosh, how long have you had it?'

'A couple of days now.'

'Do you think we ought to go back to England?'

'What good will that do?'

'I don't know. You'd feel safer in England wouldn't you, back home?'

'Well no, I don't think so. You don't feel safe anywhere with a black tongue.'

'No, I suppose not. Perhaps it was something you ate?'

'Well I've eaten almost exactly the same as you.'

'That's true, that's true.'

'*You* haven't got a black tongue by any chance, have you?'

'I don't know.'

'You don't *know*!'

'Well no, I don't know. I mean, you just don't go looking

97

at every bit of yourself every day just to see if it's gone black do you?'

'Well no; you'd have noticed though wouldn't you, in the bathroom when you cleaned your teeth?'

'Of course . . . you wouldn't care just to check for me, would you?'

'Of course.'

I stick my tongue out for Tubby's inspection just as the waiter arrives with the omelettes. He stands half-amazed, half-curious at what's going on. I quickly swallow my tongue and pick at a piece of bread. The waiter goes away and whispers to another waiter in French the equivalent of, 'We do get 'em at this time of the year, don't we.' They both look sideways at us. I wonder if they saw Tubby's black tongue. I feel quite self-conscious about it. Well, I'm his friend. A black-tongued man's friend; the friend of a freak; a freak's friend! Yes, but what of the poor freak? No wonder he's been quiet. I can assure you a black tongue is a very frightening thing to behold. After all, the tongue is part of the health barometer. What does the dear old doc do when you tell him you don't feel quite up to the mark? He feels your pulse, takes your temperature, then pulls down the corner of your eye, considers the baleful stare you give him and then, 'Yes, let's have a look at your tongue eh. Mmmm, not as clear as it might be. Mmmm, how's the old inside mmmm? Yes well, it's nothing much—you feel a bit sluggish do you? Yes soon clear that up.'

Well, if a tongue that's not as clear as it might be makes you feel sluggish, how on earth do you feel with a tongue that's as black as a bowler hat?

'How do you feel?'

'Oh, I feel all right.'

'Mmm, you see if you had blackwater fever or the black death you'd be feeling awful by now.'

'I suppose I would.'

'Ever had it before?'

''Course not!' Tubby is indignant.

'Perhaps it's the sea air or something.'

'You haven't got a black tongue, you're by the sea; all the

trippers scrambling about this lump of rock are by the sea!'

'True, well we must go to a doctor.'

'Look, give it a couple more days then I'll do something.'

'We could go back to England.'

'No, let's go and have a look at some of the old châteaux, mustn't let it spoil the holiday.'

'All right.'

And we turn inland and drive through Rennes and Saumur to the valley of the Loire. But I must say I feel a little uneasy driving further and further away from home with a man with a black tongue. Of course we can't forget it. When we book in at hotels we give our names, addresses and passports, but little does the innocent receptionist know that the holder of that passport has a black tongue. We wander through the streets of Rennes, through crowds of busy shoppers, but little do they realise they have rubbed shoulders with a man with a black tongue. We watch the French cavalry trotting the elegant broad roads of Saumur, dignified, proud, aristocratic and blind—blind to the fact that they are trotting past a man with a black tongue. One of the horses' tongues, sloppy with saliva, lolls from the side of its mouth. Tubby staring at it absolutely riveted. It's a sort of piebald tongue, pink and blotched pale purple.

'You didn't catch your complaint from a horse, did you Tubby?'

'Huh! There are animals with black tongues aren't there?'

'Oh yes, er, chow dogs they have black tongues, well no, they're purple really, but parrots now their tongues *are* black and snakes of course, some snakes' tongues are beautifully black. Quick as lightning too.'

'All right, all right. Where are we going today?'

Well, you can practically drive at random in this part of the world. You're never very far away from a lazy river that has all the time in the world to glide through the lush country. You are never very far away from a fairy-tale château that has set itself in just the right place to protect a town high on a hill or to wallow in luxury beside an olive green river. The rivers Loire, the Vienne, Cher and Indre have whiled away centuries and centuries of time here, and are never bored by the listless life. They've lent their lethargy to the heavy Charolais cattle, to the tall swaying reeds, to the quivering larch trees, to the fisherman who sits in perfect peace humped on a stool, his line drifting slowly towards a stone bridge that takes the river in three most graceful strides. The sun shines so gently behind a thin film of clouds. A breeze huffs a puff of dust through the cow-parsley, and lunch is not too far away. There is no urgency, no rush. We haven't to be anywhere at any specific time. It's so pleasant to drive slowly.

The luxury of slow motoring I don't believe has been fully explored. We slowly roll the roads and arrive at the château at Azay-le-Rideaux. Like many of the châteaux here it was put in position during the Renaissance, placed carefully beside a lake so that it can look at itself all day long and admire its rounded turrets, moulded pale grey stone, appreciate its smart cone turret hats hammered in dark blue slate polished in the sun like burnished gun metal. Of course it's a dream, our dream of a perfect life, of heaven. This is what life should be like, all lovely and grand and beautiful where you can gaze from the elegant carved windows across the dark water to the green trees, and think of your great power and strength in your castle. Where you can float down the wide easy stairs thinking lovely thoughts, only nice thoughts naturally, of how you can appear to be good and qualify for eternity.

That's the thought, of course. The thought that built the château. The reality is that we in no way measure up to these lovely thoughts. For the châteaux were squabbled about, fought over and slaughtered upon for possession of a lovely powerful thought. They were built and possessed by tyrants, land grabbers, money grubbers, the dominant, clever and ruthless. But at least they have left us something to look at. They employed architects who had eyes and craftsmen who had hands. And they left us something to look at. A lovely symbol of what life ought to be like for all of us. That's the trouble with modern tyrants, they are so abysmally greedy and mean. They leave us nothing, nothing, nothing but concrete junk.

'Wouldn't it be nice if some of our tycoons built us something to look at?'

'Yes, not much hope though,' said Tubby.

No, not much hope. No, the days of the tyrants with taste have gone. Let's go and look at what some of the other old rascals did.

It's not very far from Azay-le-Rideaux to Villandry, a few kilometres, and we do it in the record slow time of three hours—that included lunch of course. The château at Villandry is remarkable for its garden. Just walking about in the garden along the narrow gravel paths means nothing at all. You have to get up above the garden to appreciate it. And of course there is a high terrace with a stone balustrade where you can view the splendours of this most articulate and precise garden. For it was planned, one imagines, on paper: a geometrical garden of triangles, circles and squares and then executed just like that. And executed it was, for it is a dead garden in a way; acres of geometric shapes, of neat clipped box hedges surrounding round, square and triangular blobs of marigolds and poppies. The tyrant in charge here wanted order and by jingo he got it! It's like a fine piece of geometric embroidery. Even the vegetable garden is arranged to stand to attention in platoons. But cabbages and cauliflowers look more at home boxed in with little box hedges all ready for market.

It is the most formal of all formal gardens. A garden where the formalities and proper behaviour of the drawing room are carried with dignity to the garden. You feel that the garden is never weeded, it's dusted.

'Anne-Marie, have you dusted the ballroom?'

'Oui, monsieur.'

'Have you done the boudoir?'

'Oui, monsieur.'

'And the dungeons?'

'Oui, monsieur.'

'Then please to go and dust the garden.'

It's not very far from Villandry to Chenonceau and we do it in a record slow time of several hours. We get there at the end of the day. Chenonceau is lots of people's favourite château, and it's nice to have a favourite château—why shouldn't you? It's a beautiful château, for it spreads its easy elegance right across the river Cher. On stone arches that leap one after the other across the water, stands the long gallery of the château, and on the bank the glorious hunks of stone and turret still command the river and the land around as they have since the sixteenth century. The amusing thing about Chenonceau is that its building was begun in the early sixteenth century by none other than a tax collector. Which all goes to show that it's no good getting yourself a nice cushy job if you don't know how to use it. Nevertheless it also goes to show that it's more satisfying to have your money filched away from you, and diverted and converted into a shining château than have it hacked away from you to disappear into the pit of waste and squander. If you ever feel like it and can manage it, may I recommend that you go to Chenonceau in the late afternoon when the sun is getting down in the heavens a bit. The bulk of the trippers have gone. A few people wandering in the gardens, formal gardens but of a free and easy nature quite unlike the tense constricted gardens of Villandry. A couple of white swans come sailing up stream. This is their river, it is their castle. The housemartins chortle and burble and skim low over the water. Housemartins? Châteaumartins I suppose they should be around here. Yes, châteaumartins.

We wander around the gardens back to the main entrance. A party of Italians come tumbling out of the château and make for their coach, the only coach left. They are chattering, laughing, without a care in the world, hahahah, hahahah. Little do they know that they are being watched most enviously by a man with a black tongue. Oh yes, every now and again the black tongue gloom slinks up on Tubby and he falls pensive and silent.

'Look, there's bound to be a doctor in the town. Shall we go and get his advice?'

'All right.'

We go up into the town but the doctor, it seems, is not here today. But now that we've started let's try the chemist. You know, chemists are very knowledgeable; this one might know in a tick, there may be a lot of black tongue going about. We go into the chemist's. Oh they're bound to have something here. Great coloured jars and bottles billow all over the shelves, ah, but there's no chemist. Just a young girl who by the look of her in normal circumstances is frightened of life, very frightened of life. She is alone in the shop it seems, and when I say, 'Do you speak English?' she goes *hooooooooo*. She is alone in the shop with foreigners. This isn't going to be easy.

These dear little girls are not as common as they used to be, but such is their timidity that they are afraid to utter. When they are forced to speak the breath just escapes from their lungs and puffs by the vocal chords without twanging them. So that if you say to them, 'Would you like a nice slice of chocolate cake my dear?' they say, 'No thanks, I'd rather have a doughnut.' This one here would rather have a doughnut. She's not going to say a dickie bird.

Now Tubby's French is not extensive, it's just oui, non, bonjour, merci. Mine is not much more. Now then let's see, it's often better to take a run at it.

'Bonjour Mademoiselle, mon ami ici a un langue noir.'

Well that's near enough surely, my friend here has a black tongue. Her eyes are wide her nostrils distended—god, oh god, please help me, please help me.

'Better show her your tongue, Tubby.'

Tubby sticks out his tongue. He might have dropped his trousers. Rather-have-a-doughnut sways in terror towards the bath salts. And then her plea to heaven is answered, the good Lord sends her enough strength to spin around and belt off into a back room.

'Gone to get a bottle of something, I expect.'

'Huh.'

Two minutes later the door of the back room opens and there stands the chemist. He is a very dark and hairy chemist—he is also a livid chemist. He's in a rage. *Letendraiment*: what the devil do you mean coming in here frightening this poor girl to her death, *letendraiment*, if this is some sort of a joke then you can play him somewhere else, I will show you . . . He's coming to pitch us out of his shop, *letendrai*. Look out!

I must say Tubby played it beautifully. Like a confident cricketer who's seeing the ball well and playing the fast bowling with ease. As the maddened chemist rounded the corner by the baby foods Tubby let him have it. Right in line with his delivery he slipped out one black tongue, dead in the chemist's angry vision. He stopped in his tracks and went back half a pace. He had half a mind to run. Mon dieu, mon dieu. His face is a study. The rage fading away and incredulity creeping up.

Once again Tubby plays it his way. He moves towards the chemist with his black tongue sticking out, saying: 'I've got a black tongue, there you are, a black tongue!'

The chemist has never seen anything like it. Rather-have-a-doughnut hides behind the toothbrushes. The chemist does not know what to say. He can only lift his shoulder, raise his arms and go: 'Huhuhu, encore, encore!'

'He wants an encore, Tubby.'

Tubby does him a nice long encore.

'Hehehehahahah.' And then the chemist has an idea. He turns Tubby around and punches him in the kidneys. Feel anything? He punches him in the small of the back, he spins him around and punches his chest, his stomach. He punches him all over. Feel anything? No. Hahahah, a man of extremes, this chemist. Hopping mad one minute, laughing like a drain the next. We can just about understand the questions he asks. What foreign lands had we visited? Did he smoke? Had any of the family suffered from black tongue? And then a brilliant question: did Tubby work in a coal mine?

I can't help feeling he hasn't a clue what's the matter with Tubby. Not that he didn't try to find out. Never has anyone done so much and learned so little. Still, try these. Might do something. He hands Tubby a tube of pills, name of something-something-something-mycin.

'Oh that'll do it! Anything with mycin is very reassuring, I mean if you've got anything with mycin in that'll knock it.'

'Will it?'

'Oh yes.'

'I wonder, I wonder.'

And then as we drive away a silence gradually settles down.

'Let's have some lunch, shall we?'

'Yes, and a couple of bottles of red wine.'

'Yes, a couple of bottles of red wine, that's what I feel like.'

And so we have lunch and a couple of bottles of red wine.

'It's the only thing to do, get slightly blotto, it's the only way that I can forget the affliction,' says Tubby sadly.

Little did we know as we drank the deep red wine that it and it alone was the cause of Tubby's black tongue. Because when we got back home after a couple of days Tubby's tongue became normal again. No red wine. And we had to come home to find that out. 'Mid pleasures and châteaux there's really no place like home.

CHAPTER NINE

Escaping the Package Tour

The package holiday must surely be counted as one of the great blessings of this age. It has helped so many to see so much, to eat such a lot, to get so brown, to feel so ill, to laugh a lot and drink a drop, and scatter the money all over the world. Quite incredible is the package holiday. A masterpiece of cut-price organisation. What would we do without it? And yet of course all the blessings have their curses to go with them. Well, you couldn't have a blessed package holiday if it weren't for those cursed jet aeroplanes.

But of course you don't have to go by jet to go on a package tour, you can go by coach, and the package coach-tour is undoubtedly a blessing. Ten days abroad visiting five different countries, all in with your tea—for how much? Oh, a modest wage claim would cover it. But a blessing though the package coach-tour may be for the package tourer, it carries with it curses for others. For every package coach-load that tumbles into an hotel at night there are some individual travellers wandering around looking for somewhere to lay their weary heads.

Had you forgotten the individual traveller? Yes, the freelance milestone inspector. The one who likes an unorganised meander, who cares not much where he goes, save that it is where he wants to go, *when* he wants to go. There are still some individual travellers about but they are threatened with extinction; you can put him on the list along with the Bengal tiger and the blue whale, and if these two formidable mammals can't adjust to changing conditions, heaven help the poor individual traveller in his little corduroy cap. He's on the way out. It's his fault of course for being an individual traveller. His nocturnal territories are being ruthlessly poached and over-run by the block-bookers. He simply cannot exist against the big block-booker. For the big block-booker books in very big blocks, and the individual traveller should abandon his silly little ways and join the big block-booked parties.

For things are no longer as they used to be for individual travellers on the continent. In the dear dead days as the sun went down and twilight tip-toed softly down the fearful foreign mountains, two individual travellers (Tubby Foster and I) would chance upon a wayside inn, a friendly light glowing from a window, a vigorous wood fire cracking in the hearth, a smell of—*mmm*—something subtle drifting from the kitchen. The landlord, looking like a suet dumpling, comes rolling towards us.

'Good evening, gentlemen, you are looking for some accommodation?'

'Well, yes we are.' I reply and then whisper to Tubby, 'It's fantastic, he realises we're English!'

'Yes, I don't know how they do it! Just looking at me I wouldn't know I was English.'

'Yes, vell, ve still have some quite nice rooms. Ve have tonight staying here a French family, and some people from Luxembourg, an Italian couple and now two Englishmen, such a mixture ya?'

'Yes, such a mixture.'

'Now, for the eating tonight we are having the blue trout.'

'Blue trout!'

'Ya, and ve are having wenison.'

'Wenison!'

'Ya, wenison, you are liking wenison?'

'Oh yes, yes very much. Is it in a sort of stew or something?'

'Stew, nein nein, ze wenison is zoaked in vine.'

'Wenison in vine.'

'Ya, vis wenison vis vine and with herbs and then after two days in ze vine is taking out and wrapping with pastry and roasting.'

'Wrapping with pastry and roasting . . .'
'Ya, wrapping and roasting.'
'Mmmmm . . .'
'But if you don't vant, then we have some vunderful weal.'
'Vunderful weal . . .'
'Ya, vunderful weal.'
'Vunderful weal and wenison in vine. Mmmm. What do you think, Tubby, weal or wenison?'
'Job to say.'
'Ja, vis the weal you can having it many different ways . . .'
I won't go on, for the torment and despair of any species facing extinction is intolerable if it persists in living in the past. Does the blue whale dream of the days before margarine and lipstick? No no, it thrashes on and tries to forget. And so the individual traveller struggles on, even though times are changing too fast for him. The block-booker is winning hands down.

'We'd better think about getting somewhere to stay,' Tubby suggests.
'Yes, I suppose we had.'
'Not much hope of chancing upon a wayside inn.'
'No, better make for the next town—the book says there are four hotels there. Pick the biggest, the 300-bedder.'

Now we have managed to get into this sort from time to time. It's just like a squared-up beehive of 600 concrete cells, 300 bedrooms with 300 bathrooms and lavatories attached. The glasses in the bathroom are wrapped in sterilised crackly hygienic paper. The lid of the lavatory wears an ambassador's sash of paper saying sterilised. It is meant to impress, as ambassadors' sashes do. A paper sash on a lavatory seat: the seal of quality and integrity. The inference, of course, is that you've got a fresh loo. You are the first, nobody else has, untouched by human—well, it's a proud moment for you, pity to spoil it really.

And that's how you feel about it. 'I do wish they wouldn't put these cigar bands on the lavatory.'
'I know, I think it's terrible the way you rip them off, very ruthless of you.'
'It's like some awful opening ceremony.'

108

'Contamination ceremony! You might just say a few words, you know: have much pleasure in declaring this doings open, and I'll second it later on.'

Nevertheless, this sort of hotel is adequate if you can get it. It's exactly the same as every other new hotel that's built nowadays. Just a squared-up beehive. Not worth wasting one's indignation on the fallen architect who went soliciting for this sordid bit of work. Forget the outside, come inside. Plate-glass doors suck silently apart as you walk into what they call the entrance hall. It's like walking into Hell. The most violent and dreadful dungeon of Hell kept specially for the murderous, the wicked and those that do nasty things to the weak and helpless. Oh, the devil teaches them a lesson here. For the devil is an interior decorator and makes us suffer for our sins, with a black and red striped carpet, one wall a muddy navy blue, another wall of green slime, another of orange and yellow dots and a black ceiling spewing down copper tubes whence cometh just enough light to make us aware of the horror of our situation. If architects and their sponsors are indifferent to the human race then some interior decorators must hate us with a terrible hatred.

'Huh, can I help you please?'

'Oh yes, have you any accommodation for the night?'

'Accommodation? I don't think so, but please wait a moment.'

'Funny, could have sworn this place was practically empty?'

Yes, there's no one about—just one little page-boy demon on the far side of Hell lounging by the lift that takes you down to the furnace. Then a couple of enormous coaches pull into the forecourt, and the place begins to buzz. Two coachloads of bees come buzzing in, one coachload of French bees and one coachload of German bees. Suitcases start thumping about. The French bees buzz around their suitcases, *bzbzbzbzbzbz*. The German bees around theirs, *Ichhabenich-tainossenschlossen*.

Then the French bees buzz over to the reception desk where we are waiting, *bzbzbzbzbzb*. The clerk is still going over his list.

'I'm sorry, we are completely full.'

Bzbzbzbzbzbz. The hive belongs to the bees. The block-booked bees. Well, of course it was designed for them. It's simply a feed-and-sleep factory. They come in at seven o'clock for dinner at eight-thirty. Block-booked dinners, all the same, no messing about with 'What would you like, medium or rare?' There you are—get on with it. And they are all in bed by half past ten. Well they've got to, because the coach leaves at six the next morning.

Who wants to cater for individual travellers? They are a nuisance, they dare to have preferences, they come and go as they please. You don't know where you are with individual travellers but with block-bookers, oh they're lovely, block-bookers, no trouble at all.

And so you see what a joy it is for the individual traveller to find himself in a country where there are lots of hotels too small for the block-booker to block book. Switzerland, beautiful Switzerland! It's over 100 years since Mr Thomas Cook organised his first small touring party to Switzerland. Little groups travelling by train, by horse and on foot and staying overnight high in the Alps in pretty fretwork hotels. Those hotels are still there, still there for the convenience and comfort of the individual traveller.

And if you want to follow the River Rhine from source to mouth you need to be an individual traveller. Now the River Rhine rises in the Alps. Well, it doesn't really rise—it sinks or slips or slithers. Because as far as we can make out the Rhine starts off as little beads of perspiration, the sweat of the towering mountains, the sweat that begins to ooze in the spring and then trickle as the sun warms a bit of life into the world and the heavy coat of winter snow begins to moult away. That beautiful pristine fleece gets tattered and shaggy and soggy as the sweat streams out of the hem. And now in later summer the water gurgles in the valleys and burnishes the boulders as it bounces out of control, not knowing or caring where it's going. And the tremendous mountains look grey and exhausted, scraggy, gaunt and itchy. Very itchy with bits of old snow stuck in the shoulder blades and behind the ears.

'Those mountains look as though they could do with a good scratch don't they, like a lot of old tramps that have been sleeping rough?' I say.

'Yes, it's amazing that the snow lasts so long.'

'Mmmm.'

I doubt if it will all be out of the way before the fresh lot comes flying in, although on a day like this it's difficult to imagine anything quite as outrageous as a blizzard. It's a great big alpine day. A rare day now, when the world seems vast, beautiful and pure. A real day to give the lungs a treat. Oh they haven't filtered anything like this for a long time—not a cough or a backfire in it, such a change from the corroding fumes of the cities, the crisp thin air of the mountains. The sun hanging in a clear, pale sky, the rocky mountains standing naked to the waist and from their massive middles a wonderful skirt of dark green trees sweeps right down to blue pools, still and reflective. And just piercing through the trees the white needle spire of a wooden church and the ting-tang of a bell. Tang tang tang, distant but so clear, tang tang tang. Tanged out in the hollow sound-box of an alpine valley. Tang tang tang, the sound ripples around like rings on a pond, tang tang tang.

It's not the church bell in the spruce forest, it's the bell on the neck of a meandering cow as she moves on to the next mouthful, tang tang tang. Must be strange to have your dinner registered by a tell-tale bell. Tang tang, three chips, tang tang, half a mushroom, tang tang, a lump of steak, tang tang, much too big, tang, for your mouth to deal, tang, delicately with, tang tang, glug, tang phew, clanged up a few decibels there! A few peas now I think, tang tang, and a half a glass of Nuits St George, ding ding ding tang. Only a fool would try the celery. Go on then, try. Crrk, tang, crrk, tang, crrk, tang. You'd deafen yourself if you ate too much celery and you'd have to hold yourself in check with the broad beans too—hic, tang, hic, tang, hic, tang.

'You know Tubby, I think the best way to slim would be to tie a bell around your neck.'

'Mmmm, you'd cheat, wouldn't you?'

'Yes, beat the curfew and hang on to the clapper.'

'Come on, we can't sit here all day.'

I know, it's like sitting in a picture. Just the cowbell, tang tang, and the baby brook dribbling, slobbering to itself, blblblblb.

'You know, I've got a feeling that the scenery can't get any better, it can only get worse,' I say.

'Well, we'd better find out.'

'Right!'

It's no trouble to find the Rhine of course, once it gets to any sort of size. It's clearly marked on the map—the Hinter Rhein—and a fine mountain road bowls along beside it. But the scenery doesn't get any better for suddenly, and it happens very suddenly in the Alps, the scenery gets blotted out by rain. And it rains and rains and rains. We drive through the grey gloom, and everything is dull and deadened with rain and fog.

I don't know how long we sat in this foggy trance, but I am suddenly aware that I have in my hand a table napkin. A linen table napkin, well I think it's linen and it's beautifully embroidered in one corner. Funny how a bit of embroidery can bring you back to life. I remember we stopped at this little restaurant, dashed in out of the rain and were given a table by the window. It's quite an ordinary little restaurant—medium sort of prices on the menu, one or two human shapes hunched over a bowl of this and a plate of that, a waitress tinkling with spoons and forks in the corner and the rain weeping down the window. And then I noticed the table napkin. And *then* the table cloth.

'Tubby we've got a table cloth!'

'Yes, we had one yesterday.'

I know, but that was a rather posh establishment, this is an ordinary little restaurant, but every table is draped with crisp embroidered table cloths and dotted with well-ironed table napkins. The knives and forks are polished and bright, a waitress stands beside us wearing a pretty pink dress and a white apron that is scalloped and scrolled and smothered with embroidery, embroidery so delicate and precise, so pretty and intricate.

There stands thousands of hours of concentrated care.

The little steel needle has left its track all over that glorious apron. A decorated diploma for organised nervous energy. Probably the most effective form of occupational therapy ever devised, to sit and fiddle with a needle, the attention riveted on one square millimetre of space and be able to talk at the same time. Ah, that was the important bit. The talking. I remember very often the best needlewomen were the best talkers, or at least the most prolific talkers. Never still or quiet for a minute the bright needle towing a line of shining silk in and out, down and up, down and up . . . 'So I said, I said it's not a bit of use you coming to me like that, I warned you time and time again and so has your Uncle William, you can't expect us to keep on putting our hands in our pockets, we can't afford it. Where do you think the money's coming from? I said. Well, that was on the Wednesday and she never came near the place until the following Tuesday—no, it was Monday because I was getting ready to go over to grandfather's—well, I said, you might have let us know you were coming, I said, but not a word, not a word . . .' And the needle pricked and the silk dipped down and up, down and up.

Oh yes, a lot of family history was stitched into the embroidery, you can almost hear it talking. If only there was trickle of words. That's the fascinating thing about hand embroidery, you can almost here it talking. If only there was a machine that could play it back. I know the raging scandals in some of my aunt's table runners would be enough to set the West of England on fire, and the pretty wit in cousin Helen's cushion covers would keep us giggling all day. That's why embroidery is so very touching.

I'm sorry to keep on about it but Switzerland is full of embroidery. All the waitresses in this little restaurant, all the table cloths and napkins, all decorated with hand embroidery. The work that we value so highly, the work of the hand—hand embroidery, hand-carved wood. The restaurant is hand carved, hand decorated and painted. The work of the hand.

Switzerland is packed full with intricate hand work. Quite possibly the brutal aspect of the mountains compels people

113

to design and decorate, to flounce and frill and chip and bodger. You need something to offset the grey shale hunchbacks and the cold dispassionate snow. Or perhaps you just need something to do? But really you need something to look at. Just consider the decorated villages we've passed through. There was Werdenberg, a mediaeval village with a castle, a cluster of houses, a lake of glass stuck with ducks—unbelievable place. Some of the houses were carefully decorated with rambling leaves in painted panels, some faced with tiny wooden tiles—beautiful tiles, cut from the wood, biscuit-thin, shaped like the scales of a fish. There they lurch and totter, the ancient houses of Werdenberg, plastered in prettiness and fish skin with geraniums sticking out of their ears. It is quite difficult to believe that it still exists.

What has saved it goodness only knows, but somehow it has survived the plague. All towns get the plague nowadays. Ring a ring of roses, a street of lovely houses, tishoo tishoo, all knock down. But it hasn't been knocked down. A most glorious cobble of hand work.

'I say, Johnny, do you see that chap up there?'

'Yes, he's waving to us isn't he?'

'Yes, I think so.'

But as we get nearer we see that he's not waving to us, he's grooming his cow, great sweeping arm movements over the cow's back and under the belly, the cow standing still with a vacant smirk on its face.

'Nice to have enough time to clean a cow like that,' says Tubby.

'Well, perhaps he's had his motor car stolen—got to clean something! Do you think that's his missus over there?' On a very steep slope above us an old, old woman rocks herself down the hill sweeping a great scythe in front of her. She's done this ever since she was a buxom lass, what, sixty years ago? Scything down the hillside and walking back up again, taking a bit of old sharpening stone out of the pocket in her pinny, *tooweetooowee*, wiping a sharp shine on the scythe's cutting edge. And she ticktocks back down the hill again, her bony elbows see-sawing and the old wicked scythe swishing to her steady rhythm and the astonished grass falling helpless. She turns again at the bottom of the hill and walks slowly back up. She knows that she'll have to do it about sixty-five more times before the field is finished. And yet as her old splayed boots plod the slope you can't help thinking that this might be her very last turn. But out comes the sharpening stone, *tooweetoowee*. She stands sideways on to us, Old Mother Time sharpening her scythe, bent with toil, shrivelled with age, in her old faded frock and headscarf, a headscarf so big wrapping up her little head, for all we can see of her is the tip of her nose sticking out with the sun on it. *Tooweetoowee*, and she's off again down the hill, the grass toppling over just in front of her.

'Have you ever tried to use a scythe, Tubby?'

'Yes.'

'How did you get on?'

'Nearly lost a couple of legs.'

'Yes, you would never cut a slope like this with a tractor.'

'Oh no.'

No, it has to be done by hand—the dear old hand work. Some would say that they're still living in the past here. Yes, some would; and you *can* live in the past here—take for instance Baden Baden. Gentle reader, if ever you get a chance, go to Baden Baden and have tea at the Kurhaus. Now I'm not much of a one for tea and cream cakes but the show that's put on for one and all has to be seen to be believed. Baden Baden was of course a most fashionable place to go to take the waters. A place where the money flowed as freely as the spa water, money that tumbled in from all over the world and built the casino like a glittering royal palace—expansive terraces, glorious gardens, and a high, domed bandstand. All the crowned heads of Europe came to Baden Baden. King Edward VII of England took his crown off when he came here, and bought himself a homburg hat from nearby Homburg where they are made. Oh yes, you came to Baden Baden if you were someone someone.

And do you know, they are still playing out the old

charade. Yes, just look at the long terrace in front of the casino, several hundred choice tables with people taking tea. A real orchestra, a big orchestra of about forty players playing a Strauss waltz—fledermaus, tralalal. People are strolling past the flower beds, bowing to one another, smiling, the gentlemen with ladies on their arms dressed in their very best. You can hardly believe it. Look at that tall elegant man with a brown bowler hat, a pearly grey suit and spats. *Spats.*

'I haven't seen a spat for years, have you?' I asked.

'No, spats went out when plus fours came in—you couldn't wear the two together.'

'It looked silly. Care for a cup of tea?'

'Yes, I think so.'

And we sit on the terrace in the sun and order tea, tralalala.

'How do you feel?'

'Very peculiar,' said Tubby.

Yes, it's odd to drop into an era that is really dead and gone. For we are sitting right in the middle of the second decade of this century, in the middle of a glorious social show-off. All the ladies wearing wedding hats and christening hats, well hung with jewellery and carrying sunshades. Look at the refined lady at the next table, in a tussore silk dress trimmed with black velvet. She is considering a plate of cream cakes set before her. She slowly peels away her long elegant gloves and lifts her veil back over her marshmallow hat. I haven't seen anyone do that for years. The cakes now have free access to her face. Tralalalalal.

'Pity that the past was so good for some and so rotten for others.'

'Yes. They can't go on living in the past like this, can they?'

'They'll try to.'

Tralalala. 'We are just as bad you know.'

'How do you mean?'

'Well, we moan about the package tours and the block-bookers block-bookings all the hotels.'

'Yes I know.'

116

Oh yes, the past was all right for some, rotten for others—nevertheless it is nice when things *are* nice to be living in the past. Very nice indeed.

CHAPTER TEN

Nightlife in Lion City

It's very difficult to describe a city or a place in a few concise sentences. Unless of course someone asks you what such-and-such a place is like and you can honestly say absolutely ghastly. Still doesn't describe the place accurately. And I've always found it very difficult to get a clear picture of Singapore from the chaps that I've met on leave in the mother country.

You ask them, 'What is Singapore like?'

'Oh Singapore, well it's fascinating.'

'In what way?'

'Oh I don't know really, it's sort of got a bit of everything you know.'

'What's a bit of everything?'

'Oh well, you know, you've got Chinese, Malays, Indians, Pakistanis, Eurasians, Europeans all mixed up together.'

'Yes, but what sort of a place is it to live?'

'Oh, it's a wonderful life, a wonderful life.'

'Oh I see, sounds fascinating.'

That's what he said in the first place. Your questions have become as ineffectual as his answers. And even when you are lucky enough to actually get to Singapore it's still quite a job to get a clear picture of the place in one quick glance.

'How long have we been here, two days is it?' Tubby asks.

'Yes.'

I think we have learned more about Singapore from Mr Lee, the owner of our hotel. Mr Lee is Chinese, speaks excellent English, is devoted to England and all things English. He insists we dine with him each evening.

118

'Now gentlemen, I hope you will enjoy what I have prepared for you this evening. First of all I have a very special chicken soup—it is steamed in a coconut for four hours. I think you will like it.'

A coconut is put in front of us, full of steaming rich chicken soup permeated with the scent and flavour of coconut. 'To be taken slowly,' says Mr Lee, 'with a dry French white wine.' The mixture of aromas and flavours is absolutely exquisite. And we sip the soup and listen to Mr Lee, his good-tempered face smiling in the soft candlelight. It hangs there in the gloom like a crafty benevolent moon. You have got to listen to Mr Lee. Singapore, it seems, has grown faster and bigger than practically anywhere else in the world. It is of course an island. It's about 26 miles across and 14 miles from top to bottom. The Malay peninsular is less than a mile away and the equator drags its imaginary line around the world's belly about 85 miles to the south. It's a nicely placed island. It's always warm. Temperatures are never below 75° and never much above 90° so they say, but it seems a whole lot hotter than that because the atmosphere is very humid. The rains come and go as they please, they have no definite timetable, they can be light, medium or heavy enough to drive your pith helmet hard down over your ears. But the great thing about this pleasant island is that it is never blown inside out by hurricanes and typhoons.

And so it was that to these parts centuries ago came a certain prince. He was looking for a place to found a city of his own. What a lovely thing to be able to do, found a city of your own. The chap who found Birmingham has got something to answer for . . . Anyway this prince found that he could found his city on this island. It was known in those days as Tumasik, Sea Town, but he wasn't mad about the name Sea Town, there were hundreds of sea towns about. Strangely enough one day he was out with his attendants when they came upon a large strange animal. 'Good gracious,' said the prince, 'what on earth's that animal?' for he had never seen anything like it before and neither had anyone else, but some smooth bootlicker in the royal party said it was a lion. It was a pretty wild guess one imagines as lions are not exactly found in these parts. Anyway, the prince had found a name for the city he had found. Singa pura. Lion City. Lion City had its ups and downs of course but it really began to prosper when Thomas Stamford Bingley Raffles came along early in the nineteenth century and did some very smart negotiating which allowed the East India Company to trade there. It was a time of great prosperity, and Lion City grew and grew. Mr Lee turns his history lesson into a sort of fairy story. 'And now, gentlemen, it is late—what do you do in the morning?'

'Well, we thought about going to a crocodile farm.'

'Crocodile farm, yes yes, it is interesting, quite interesting.'

The next morning is a real Singapore morning. It's like living in a vast greenhouse. The big tropical house at Kew is like this, hot, humid and heavy scented. The ground is moist and charged with tremendous energy, an energy that will explode the merest speck of seed and send it soaring like a green rocket up to the blue sky and the billowy steamy cloud. An energy that generates the big burst of coconuts and cascades of bananas. An energy that transforms itself to touch off the delicate orchid.

Orchids grow in the gardens in Singapore like we grow sweet peas, in lines and up sticks. The pale and complicated orchid. They say that you have to be a gardener and a psychiatrist to grow orchids. Poor twisted, mixed-up little flowers that they are. In England I've sometimes looked a lonely orchid straight in the face and wondered what maladjustment in childhood produced that haunting expression, what repressions and jealousies gave it those tortured features. But when you see the orchids of Singapore growing like sweet peas up sticks with kids playing and dogs barking all around them you realise what gay and beautiful things they really are. They need people, a lot of activity around them to take them out of themselves. They brood and mope, that's their trouble when they are on their own. But here of course the climate's just right for orchids.

There sits our taxi driver under the frangipani tree. He waits for us every morning under the frangipani tree.

'Where you go sir?'

'Er, crocodile farm.'

'Clockodile farm, yes sir.'

He is quite an extraordinary man. He sees everything, he hears everything, he misses nothing. When he saw us first he knew he was on to a pretty good thing. We hired him for the whole day. Next day he was waiting for us. We were worth waiting for, a whole day's hire! And he is well worth his hire. He never leaves us when we go off on foot. No matter where we are, in the crowded streets, the markets, he's there just behind. We don't have to think about him. We can go up alleys, down lanes, in and out of shops, restaurants. He's there when we come out and he always manages to park his taxi within about five feet of where we meet him. Even in the crowded city. I don't know how he does it. I often look at his fantastic face and wonder what's going on in that odd-shaped nut of his.

And it is an odd-shaped nut. Like a badly knocked-about, upside-down pear. It's cropped very close so all the irregularities and odd bumps bulge out in strong relief. A phrenologist would love to have a go at his complicated cranium because he's got great mounds of brilliance, wallops of knowledge and lumps of violence swelling up all over the place. And yet the only emotion he shows is a sweet affectionate smile. It's odd to see such sweetness smiling out of such ugliness.

Now you see ugly people wherever you go all over the world. You can start with that bloke that makes faces at you in the mirror when you shave in the morning. But the ugly ones that you see in these parts are really gold medallists. It's hardly fair in a place where so many graceful and lovely ones walk, where so many lithe and trim swing along in the sun, where fine carved faces pass in droves all day long. It's hardly fair that one in every couple of hundred of these is a gold medal ugly.

They are fascinating really, because they seem to be made of spare parts. There was no proper order in their construction, no blueprint. They were shoved together, haphazard, in an old store-shed somewhere. All drawn from the storekeeper at the stores without a proper order form.

'Right, what do you want then, human being? Yes, I can make one up for you. Right, here we are, pair of legs size six, right we haven't got any size six arms—nearest we got is a pair of size eights, they'll do just as well and stretch further. Right, now I don't know, I have had them size six bodies on order for weeks—you can't get nothing nowadays can you?—look, could you manage with a size two body, doesn't look all that . . . mind you, I know . . . but then it's cheaper to run, doesn't need all that grub to keep it going. Right, now what have we got? Size two body, size six legs and size eight arms. Yes, well now, if you'd take my advice it's not worth putting an expensive head and hooter with that lot is it, waste of money isn't it? Well now, I have got a few of the old Mark Two heads left, they didn't seem to go you know. Too big for most people. Some people loved them of course, big heads, but I don't think they was all that top heavy. Nah, what we can do is balance it up a bit with a pair of 248/6 lug holes and I tell you what I'll do, I'll throw in one of those 1975 hooters free, all right? Well, they made them obsolete a couple of years ago you know, there was a lot of complaints about the down draught but there's enough clearance there, isn't there, well you know, if you keep it clean . . . Sign here, will you?'

And such a one is our taxi driver. I sit in the back of his cab looking at the back of his Mark Two head and his 248/6 ears and we arrive at the crocodile farm. Now this happened many years ago but I should have known better. Extraordinary how *one word* will lead you completely astray. The word farm is such a homely comforting word, isn't it. Well, the first things we ever mumbled as little nippers were the names of the animals in the farm book. Bow wow, bow wow; quack quack, quack quack; baa lamb, baa lamb; moo cow, moo cow. Oh dear you see how naive you can become simply because of a nostalgic word like farm. Farm. I was thinking only the nicest, simplest thoughts when we arrived at the crocodile farm: crock crock, croc, croc. Oh, I should have known better. I was simply wondering what sort of story books there would be about a crocodile farm: One morning farmer Ho Mi put on his big straw hat and his old patched smock and walked out across the fields. He was very sad because he had no money to buy food to feed his crocodiles. I'm very sorry croc crocs, he said, but you will have to go without your din dins today. Oh dear, said the croc crocs, and they all began to cry. Just then up piped little Crissy croc croc. I know, she snivelled, why not take me and turn me into a handbag then you could sell me and buy food for all the others. Oh no, said all the others, that's a terrible thing to suggest . . .

Yes isn't it? But of course a crocodile farm is simply a place where they grow handbags. And it isn't a farm at all, it's a collection of concrete pennings. Each concrete penning has a sloping floor with water at one end. And there lie the crocodiles, thick and leathery, hundreds of them, fresh water crocodiles, salt water crocodiles, they all make up beautifully. They are making them up in a room right next to the concrete pennings. Smart, last-a-lifetime handbags.

I know that not many of us have much affection for crocodiles. Their behaviour in relation to our behaviour leaves a lot to be desired. And they certainly weren't around when the good looks were handed out. But when you see hundreds of crocodiles trapped in concrete pennings just waiting to be turned into handbags you begin to feel very differently about crocodiles. You see, crocodile farms do not breed crocodiles. It's virtually impossible to provide the conditions where crocodiles breed. And so all the crocs on this farm are taken from the wild as babies. They are all baby-snatched crocs. And the wild crocodile is being snatched away towards extinction. So spare a tear for the crocodile, *his* tears are full of foreboding and he has all but shed his last.

'Well,' said Tubby, 'Mr Lee said that the crocodile farm was quite interesting.'

'Mmm, quite interesting, isn't it?'

That evening Mr Lee has to go out on business and so we go along to Albert Street to try the food there. Albert Street is noted for its eating stalls, and you can eat at them with every confidence. Gippy tummy and dysentery don't seem to live in this part of the world. I don't know why, but they don't.

The stalls are all jammed together down the side of the street. Bare electric bulbs shining white, harsh and strong over all the raw flesh, fish and poultry on offer. You can have what you like and what you like is all hung up for you to choose before it's cooked. Well, you want to know what you're going to get don't you, I mean you might get any old muck—once it's cooked you very often can't tell what it's supposed to be or what it truthfully ever was. But here it is all hung up and laid out. Chickens and ducks naked and dead, chitterlings and tripe muddled and ravelled, prawns and lobsters boiled and bucolic, bowls of gudge, dishes of fudge, jars of crrk, jugs of glong, and great pots of gippo.

They can do anything you like in Albert Street, they don't need kitchens—look, it's all cooked in those big pans at the side of the stall. Deep black pans where nothing ever sticks, nothing ever burns. Pans that are so mature, so seasoned, so old and so wise they know as much about cooking as the wizard who cooks in them. He uses a couple of large—well, I would call them paint scrapers, the sort of things you use to strip old paint off after the blow lamp. He slithers the strippers around the dishes, tossing the astonished food around, squirting in the sauces, cracking in the eggs. That chap there is cracking eggs with a hatchet, yes, but so gently; he holds the egg in one hand and taps it lightly with his hatchet and then he holds the egg to his nose. It tells him all he wants to know, whether it's good or bad. And then with one hand he shoots the egg into the pan leaving the split shell in his hand. The egg is quite prepared to settle itself down to a quiet cosy fry in the pan, but in two ticks the paint strippers are slipping about and the steam surges up beyond the electric lights, out of sight into the black night.

It's quite an education watching the cooks of Albert Street. They would be a sensation in any London restaurant cooking by your table. Imagine that bald bloke with a hatchet cooking a crêpe suzette. He'd do it with one hand. Because here he has to cook quite a lot with one hand. He has no spirit or gas stove. No, he's got a charcoal fire. And he turns out his little masterpieces over a charcoal fire with one hand. Well, with the other hand he has to fan the charcoal fire if he wants to turn up the regulator to Mark 9 and hold it there. And he stops fanning when he has to come down to Mark 3. Wonderful stuff, charcoal, it's so docile and sensitive. It responds at once to the gentlest whiff of oxygen. It blushes red and eager and the great black cooking pans pass on the charcoal's emotions at once.

Oh yes, you can do a lot worse than eat in Albert Street. Ten o'clock at night is a good time to eat and after you've eaten you can wander along to Bugis Street. You can eat in Bugis Street too if you feel like it, the food is pretty good. You can also get yourself a nice innocent game of noughts and crosses in Bugis Street or a punch on the nose. But two friends good and true are fairly safe together wandering down Bugis Street.

'Well, what about sitting here eh, and seeing what happens?' I suggest.

'Yes it's quite nice here, isn't it? What shall we have, some beer?'

'Yes, the old perspiration pumps will be disappointed if they find they've pumped themselves dry. Ah . . .' A waiter is at our table immediately. 'Two beers, please.'

'Thank you, sir.'

'Thank you. What a beautiful night it is. So bland and warm.'

'Well, I don't know about you, but I can stand any amount of this sort of existence.'

'Yes. 'Course this is the best time of the day.'

'Yes, I suppose it is. If only we had a climate like this in England things would be very different, wouldn't they? We would have a government that—hello, what do you want?' Someone is tapping me on the arm, a gentle but persistent tap. I turn and there she stands, smiling in the electric light. It's a beautiful hard little face with bright brown eyes that read the tell-tale lines on my face in a twink. She thinks I'm not bad.

'Hello mister.'

'Hello.'

'I say, careful old man.'

125

'It's all right Tubby, I can look after myself. What do you want?'

She extends a gorgeous smile. A smile that knows everything and suggests eternal happiness for one and all. There she stands, a little lady of the streets and she's only eight.

'Noughts and crosses, mister?'

'All right then, noughts and crosses.'

She carries one of those self-erasing pads and with two finger nails marks out the noughts and crosses court in a couple of swishes. You play for ten cents a game. It's an honest way of begging. Ten cents a game. Of course she wins, she wins a lot, chortling and gurgling when she know's she's going to get a line up.

There are lots of little girls in Bugis Street who are dab hands at noughts and crosses, they move around the tables playing the soldiers, sailors, civil servants and the tourists. And look at this: sauntering down through the tables is a most sensational looking girl. Hardly eighteen years old, but what a beauty and what an act she's putting on. She's like a teenage Mae West, the hips swaying away, the eyes flashing around, come up and see me sometime, heavens above! She spins around and changes direction, her long blond hair swirls around after her. She swings her handbag to the sensual movement of her firm provocative legs. It's enough to make the strongest man grip the edge of the table and try to think of England. But what chance has he got? Here comes another, a brunette equally beautiful. And another and another.

In and out of the tables of Bugis Street they parade, the most dazzling brash and beautiful bunch of les girls I have ever seen in my life. And they are not sly and suggestive, they are vivacious and pert. The sailors give them the Chai Ike—whistle whistle, oi oi. They settle here and there with groups of fellahs. A blond pauses at our table and gives us the once over. Well, well.

Gentle reader, if you wish to know the end of this strange tale I will tell you, for it is but a fact of life and it will take but a minute. But if you have already heard enough of the shady deeds of men then turn your face to the wall. For the naughty little girls that I have been telling you about are not naughty little girls at all, they are naughty little boys. Oh yes. They are well known. Are you sure? Oh yes, see the adam's apple, it's the only thing that gives them away. For they are known as the Ky Tys, the strange ones. The Ky Tys. They come from all over the place, Indonesia, Malaya, Thailand, they come here because Bugis Street tolerates their predicament and perhaps understands the lopsided mechanics of the construction. And times are changing. Aren't they indeed. The fascinating thing about the situation is this: all the chaps chatting up the Ky Tys here know perfectly well that they are men, and yet they are completely flummoxed by the sensational display of femininity that goads and titillates them. Big tough sailors all of a dither and a do-da. There are three at the next table with a wonderful brunette Ky Ty. They call her Marylad.

'Now look Marylad, what do you do about dresses? I mean do you go to a shop and try them on or what? We are just interested, you know Marylad. Yes do you make your own? Oh aren't you a clever little thing then, eee Marylad, you know Marylad you're a naughty little thing aren't you, are you naughty eh? . . .'

It's fascinating, he's holding her hand and looking at her in the soppiest way imaginable. His eyes simply will not believe what his intelligence is trying to tell him. And his intelligence is losing. His eyes are becoming more truthful every second. 'Aren't you a naughty little thing Marylad? You are, aren't you? A naughty little thing, Marylad.'

Marylad! I wouldn't have thought it possible. I know that certain members of the animal world have difficulty in recognising the opposite sex. They have to make certain tests first of all. Or else a definite display by a male convinces a female that he is a male and acceptable. But here you have a male displaying as a female and completely fooling a male who knows she's a male, if you see what I mean. It's quite astonishing. 'Where do you live then, Marylad! Come on, where do you live? I bet it's just around the corner, isn't it Marylad? Eh, just around the corner Marylad?'

'It's about time that we left I think, don't you?' said Tubby.

'Yes, I suppose it is. What's the time, one o'clock?'

'Yes, just after, and we don't want to be too late in the morning.'

'No, I don't suppose we have seen half of the place yet, do you?'

'I shouldn't think so. I'm sure there must be a lot more to see.'

Oh, I'm sure there is, but I think that for the moment we've seen enough. Perhaps a little too much.

CHAPTER ELEVEN

Lost in Sicily

It's nice to get the flavour of a place right from the start. Yes, the flavour of the place. Sicily has flavour all right—it is a great kitchen of flavours. The geography of Sicily implies that it has been kicked away from Italy as a black sheep, an outcast, the toe of the mother country caught it fair and square in the seat of its pants and booted it out into the Mediterranean. And it doesn't give a damn. It's not interested in its parentage, it's not interested in its heritage, it's a ragamuffin.

Well, that's what it appears to be. Palermo, the capital of Sicily, is a ragamuffin. The fine clothes that it once wore in the dear dead days are faded in shreds, caked with dirt and all but totally squalid were it not for the sad traces of grandeur. The cut and style of the aristocrat is still there. But what a dissolute old bounder he must have been. Completely gone to seed, immoral. A rake if ever there was one, and to Palermo one imagines all rakes progress. There must be a rakish streak in me, I fancy, for having said all that I must declare that Palermo is one of my favourite cities.

It's a bit morbid perhaps, but I have never been anywhere where the past is so utterly ignored and yet so persistently endures. Well, there are some glorious great buildings in the main streets. Eighteenth-century palaces long since abandoned by the nobles, the masonry is slipping out of place, the parapets look dangerous, the fluted columns are suffering from curvature of the spine, the stonework is stained black with age and sad from the tear stains of the rain. Grass grows in the gutters, shrubs through the roof and yet the place still lives. It's infested with people. You can't really say they live there, they infest the place, thousands of them, clattering about the courtyards, clambering up the lovely stone stairs, shouting out of the windows, hauling in the washing.

The washing, the washing! They do love the washing. These grand old courtyards are festooned with washing, like Christmas decorations in the public bar, the trimmings of the courtyards flutter all day and night.

And in the streets the horse-drawn carriages clop and plod around the decaying people's palaces. Oh yes, there must be hundreds of horse-drawn carriages in Palermo, and they are all almost as old as the rotting buildings. Yet they persist, these open carriages sagging at the springs, creaking, squeaking as they go to the rhythm of the nodding bag of bones that trots and trots the humdrum streets. They must be a hundred years old, these horse cabs. Oh yes, any museum would be pleased to put one in its entrance hall. Polished brass lamps, polished brass hubs, black-buttoned leather upholstery, collapsible black hoods like out-size perambulators, they belong to the last century, not this.

How did they survive? Well, it must have been touch and go. It only needed a couple of progressive, forward-looking modern city councillors and they would all have had the chop. But no, Sicily is a law unto itself. It lives a life of practical reality, not of calculated theory. Why scrap the horse cabs, they are so cheap? They are easy to get in and out of. And now of course Palermo couldn't do without its horse cabs, because the motor car, yes the motor car, has absolutely guaranteed them eternal life. There are so many motor cars in Palermo that it is just as quick to go by horse cab, for the pace of the traffic is just about the pace of the horse. You can go shopping in a horse cab, load up with fish and fruit, there are no doors to thwart you, there's bags of room for you and the missus and the week's groceries and you can stretch your legs right out, lean back, and of course in an open carriage you can see and you know exactly what's going on all around you. Oh yes, the old horse cab has a past, a present and a future in Palermo. And we've got the motor car to thank for that.

But that's about all we have got to thank the motor car for. In cities like Palermo the motor car is a curse and a disaster. The streets are not very wide, there don't seem to be many parking places and so cars are parked on the pavements. Yes, right across the pavements so that the poor old pedestrian is forced out into the dangerous no man's land of the street, where he's hooted at, abused and almost spat upon. But even if there is a yard or two of pavement to walk on you're not safe there. We actually saw a man knocked down on the pavement by a car jumping up the kerb to park. And now look here, right outside our hotel door is a parked car. We can scarcely get out of our own hotel. There's a swarthy driver smoking a cigarette and watching us with a dark calculating look.

'Scusi, scusi, please you speak English?'

'Yes, we do, and as you seem to be able to speak English I don't mind saying how very pleasant you motorists make life by parking on the pavements, we just can't thank you enough.'

But my sarcasm is utterly wasted. He hits straight back: 'Signor Morris, Signor Foster?

'Yes?'

'Yes?'

'Please, you want a hire car, eh?'

'Yes, but we ordered it for this afternoon.'

'Yes I know, but I think perhaps you know maybe you like to go somewhere this morning, eh where you like to go?'

'Well I don't know.' *Honk honk honk.* 'Look we're blocking the pavement and half the street.'

'Ah, that's all right, that's all right, get in get in.'

We scramble into the car. *Honk honk honk.* 'Everybody makes a lot of noise eh, we go this way.' We drop off the pavement into the street and doddle along behind a horse cab past the antique palaces, top heavy with wrought-iron balconies and washing, washing, washing. They are

131

wonderful streets, once so beautiful with affluence and now so picturesque with poverty.

'You like to have my card?'

'Oh thank you.' It says 'Guiseppe Poggioli, car hire, English spoken'. It didn't take us long to get to know Guiseppe Poggioli. He was a positive, forthright character, with quick reflexes and immediate reactions, he knew exactly what he wanted and openly fought anyone who stood in his way. We found this out in the first five minutes.

'Look is now eleven o'clock eh, what you like to do, eh, eat something, some spaghetti about half past twelve?'

'That's not much time, one hour.'

'We go to catacombs eh? You like to see the catacombs?'

'Oh well, is it far?'

'No it's just up here.' Now I have never been into a catacomb and so I just didn't know what to expect. I wasn't sure that I wanted to go into a catacomb really and so perhaps it was just as well that when we got to the catacombs the door was closed. Guiseppe Poggioli is astonished.

'Hey hey, what go on, hey what go on? What for is the door closed? That's not right, that's not right.'

'Well, I suppose it's shut sometimes.'

'Na na na, never shut always open, everybody can go in just when they want.' He struggles out of the driver's seat and goes across to the door and tries it. It's locked. He kicks it with a savage left foot, then a right, then a left. He turns to us.

'Don't worry, we get in all right, we get in.' He takes a few more indirect free kicks at the door and then a penalty and he scores! The door opens. Now we didn't know that above the catacombs there was a monastery. To get to the catacombs you go through the monastery door. And not knowing this we were astonished to see standing in the doorway in answer to Guiseppe Poggioli's penalty kick a tall monk, a long holy monk of the El Greco school with a scrawny beard trimming the fringe of his long, sad face. He held his hands as though he were threatened by a pistol, half in surrender, half in blessing. His enormous eyes forgave the world at a glance, he was obviously quite high up in the martyr class in that monastery. And perhaps it was a trick of the light but I could swear he'd got green eye shadow on his eyelids.

Goodness knows what Guiseppe Poggioli said to him, it hurt the monk terribly but he forgave him. His pale green eyelids slipped over the soft brown eyes and rolled back again. The catacombs were closed, he seemed to say. And then Guiseppe let him have another piece of his mind. It was a rotten piece and it certainly hit home for the monk suddenly flared with indignation and clutched at his chest and answered back with something that ended *so there*. But Poggioli hadn't even started yet. He knew how to deal with monks.

'Huh, look this is silly—let's find out what is the matter,' I say.

'Yes, there's going to be a fight in a minute.'

We tumble out of the car and hurry over to the argument. 'Look, what's the matter? Huh, what's the matter? What's the matter?'

And standing back, pointing an arm and forefinger at the monk, Guiseppe Poggioli denounces him. 'He lies, he's a liar, he's a liar.'

'Look, you can't go about calling monks liars.'

'Huh!' agreed Tubby.

Now whether the monk understood English or not I don't know but he granted Tubby Foster and me a most benevolent smile. I thought I heard the fluttering of dove's wings. We were totally and absolutely forgiven but that creep—his face changed in a second when he turned to Guiseppe Poggioli—that creep could go and get lost in damnation. And he slammed the door.

'Mmmmm, well what was that all about?'

'He say the catacomb is closed today, is never closed, *never*, I take everybody to the catacomb, hey everybody, is never closed. He say today is closed, he is a liar, a liar, a liar!'

'Never mind, we can go another day can't we?'

It's no good, he's a liar, a liar. They do take things to heart, these people, don't they? They do take things to heart. Guiseppe Poggioli was outraged of course, because he'd been proved wrong for once as a hire car driver, he wanted to please. He'd lost quite a bit of face.

'Never mind, you take us around somewhere.'

'Okay, don't worry. I know all the places.'

And for three days we travelled around Sicily with Guiseppe Poggioli. We were entirely in his hands, he manipulated us from one end of the island to the other. His whole attitude to life was very similar to Chico Marx of the Marx Brothers. In fact, at times it was like being in a Marx Brothers' film. And at times it was a bit alarming. There was the time when we went to visit a certain ruin. It too was closed, but Poggioli was not going to be turned away again. He found the custodian, made him open up, let us in and bow to us as we went out.

'How did you manage to get the gatehouse keeper to open up?'

'I told him you were guests of the Sicilian Regional Government and you must be permitted to go everywhere.'

'You didn't!'

'Si, why not?'

'Why not! He believed you?'

'Of course he believed me, he can't read and I show him a piece of paper. Bah!' The contempt he feels for the gatehouse keeper who can't read is obviously intended for the long monk who can. He's getting his own back on the lowly officials who guard entrances and take tickets.

But bit by bit we get accustomed to Guiseppe Poggioli's outrageous impudence. Travelling with him is like roaming the countryside as a member of a gang of confidence tricksters. He contests every obstacle and surmounts it with a string of lies, threats, winks, nudges and sometimes, but not very often, a few hundred lire as a bribe. Perhaps he's pretending that things are more difficult than they are, it's a job to say. Whenever he leaves the car he gets hold of someone right away. He draws the victim close to him, whispering in his ear, glancing towards us—the two people in the car. He's probably saying we are British Ambassadors, or royalty, or something. The victims view us with great respect. 'Si si si, scusi scusi.' Poggioli comes paddling back, his long overcoat flying out behind him, not a sign on his swarthy face as to whether he has good news or bad. His eyes flick about all over the place in case there's a couple of thousand lire lying about.

'Well, what's he say?'

'He say that hotel is closed. And that hotel is no good. They rob you, but he tell me where to go, I know.' Guiseppe Poggioli does everything. He has long discussions with reception clerks and managers of hotels. Sometimes it lasts for half an hour. We stand aside and wait. We get looked up and down and whispered about.

You know, I wonder sometimes if old Poggioli isn't telling them that we are mental or something. Well, he knows every trick in the book, wonder what he *has* told them.

'Well, what did you tell them?'

'Oh you know what, you got the best rooms in the hotel at half price.'

'What did you tell them?'

'Oh, the manager is a friend of mine.'

'*What* did you tell them?'

'Well, that you were friends of the Governor of the province, and that you do some business with citrus fruits.'

'Really?'

'Is all right—you got the best rooms half price hey?'

What can you do? Well, what you could do would be to say, Now look Poggioli, we'll attend to the hotels and things, now you leave everything to us, you see we being English don't like this underhand sort of stuff. But it wouldn't have worked. Poggioli was much too quick and fiery for us.

And then one day we saw something. Something that we can't forget. We do forget about it from time to time but then at odd moments the eyes stop seeing. They stop seeing the beach, the palm trees, the blue beautiful sea. They are wide open but not seeing, for the memory obscures the view. The memory is often much stronger than the vision it takes over. That blasted memory! You can't get rid of it. There's nothing you can do about it for once the memory has a hold

135

of you, you are compelled to sit through the whole film of that extraordinary hour or so we spent in the catacombs in Palermo. Oh yes, we did get in eventually.

I only hope that the film will wear thin or snap or get lost, anything, but there's not a hope. It's as sharp and colourful a bit of film as I have in my memory film-library at the moment. And the operator, that damned projectionist sitting up there in the back of my nut, keeps putting that film on—oh a dozen times a day. More I fancy. He's just put it on *again*.

There we go, Tubby Foster and I in an open horse carriage, clip-clop clip-clop, along one of the dark, decaying streets of Palermo. Clip-clip clop-clop. We had a couple of hours to wait before Guiseppe Poggioli came to pick us up to take us to the airport where we were to fly to Rome. Clip-clop clip-clop, oh dear there we go in that horse cab. You see, you can't stop it. We are just rounding a corner and in a second or so we will be stopping outside the catacombs. The cab driver has a very strange face. He has one very heavy eyelid that droops well down over his sad brown eye. The sash cords have gone or something, he just can't keep his left eyelid up. Of course, you haven't seen it yet. You will in a tick. *There*, he turns as he eases the cab horse to a stop and points with his whip to the door of the catacombs. See that strange face? We'll see it again when we come out but we won't take much notice of it—far too much on our minds. There you are, we are getting out of the cab, a couple of jolly chaps.

'You wait, eh, wait?'

'Si, si.'

'Won't be long, ten minutes, ten minutes.'

'Si, si.'

Very ordinary little door, isn't it, leading into a little vestibule. There's a small folding table with a saucer on it. There's a little money in the saucer and a notice on the wall saying it is for the maintenance of the catacombs. We both put some coins in the saucer. Tubby first and then me, you see. Bit hesitant perhaps—go on, another couple of hundred. That's it.

Lot of detail in this film. Nothing's missed. It's a perfect record, a wretched indelible record. We walk through the vestibule, and down some stone steps. Listen to us:

'How long do you think it will take to get to the airport?'

'Oh I don't know, what—twenty minutes?'

'Oh yes, I suppose so. Old Poggioli goes like the wind the moment we are out of the city. And it's a very good road.'

We chatter on down the steps. Now it's useless for me to say that if I'd known what was at the bottom of those steps I would never have gone down because you can't possibly know what's there until you do go down. But the film's been made, it's running through the frantic cogwheels at the back of my nut. We get to the bottom of the steps. It's gloomy, but there's a ghostly light seeping in from somewhere above. We stop.

Now I can usually stop the film here for a moment but not for long, just long enough I hope for you to switch me off if you don't wish to know what was at the bottom of those stone steps. Switch me off, because as heroes of old used to say it's not a very pretty sight. On the other hand it's an experience, an experience that is quite horrifying, but at the same time an experience that completely purges the muddled mind. And that's no bad thing. It presents a clear and absolutely simple picture of life, for here we are face to face with the obverse side of life—death.

Here we go, I can't hold the film any longer, are you coming? Into the catacombs. I don't know whether they are natural caves or if they were hewn out for the purpose, bit of both probably and I'm only guessing for there was much to occupy my mind and I didn't really investigate properly. Anyway, the catacombs are a large collection of huge caves all connected with passageways. It could be that the geological structure around Palermo is of a hard rocky nature and grave digging a difficult business, it could be that in a hot climate bodies have to be removed from the civilised world pretty quickly.

And in the past in Palermo the citizens, when they'd lived their lives and gasped their last, were brought to the catacombs. They were brought in their best Sunday suits and evening gowns. They were brought in tall top hats and velvet coats, they were brought in the finest lace and satin skirts. They were brought in workday clothes and canvas cadaverous bags. They were brought in little round hats with swinging tassels, they were brought in little mop caps and embroidered collars. They were brought in the golden robes of bishops, in the scarlet gowns of cardinals.

Year after year, to the tolling bell and the scuff of the coffin carriers' heavy tread, they were brought to the catacombs, taken from their coffins and hung upon the wall. Yes, hung upon the wall, by a wire under the arm and attached to the wall. Hung to the wall. And they are all here. *All here*. Right in front of us. Over eight thousand of them. Eight thousand, so they say. You see why the film keeps rattling through my head. As they were dressed on the day they died they were brought to these caves and just put against the walls in tiers. There's a row at floor level, a row above them in alcoves and a row above them. All dressed up dead people. Men, women and children. Dead but so horribly alive.

Well, it's the clothes, the shocking memory of the clothes, the mantle of the living still hanging upon the dead. Beautiful faded dusty clothes from the seventeenth, eighteenth and nineteenth centuries, a museum of clothes with real dead models still in them. Shrivelled, dried out, grinning models, their hats slipped down over their eyes, their knees buckled, their shoulders hunched and long claws sticking out of the cuffs. *Hahahah.* Can you wonder that we had hysterics—*hahaha*? It is a hideous horrific joke. A dreadful ghastly prank. For the longer you gaze at the dead the more alive they seem to be. Those two priests side by side, both twisted in towards one another. One is talking to the other out of the side of his mouth. 'I don't mind telling, you know, but that vow of celibacy is a load of old rubbish.' 'Don't tell me, everybody knew about you and your funny little ways *hahaha*.'

Of course we had hysterics, for about ten minutes I suppose. Why didn't we turn tail and bolt? I don't know. I don't know. We staggered from cave to cave convulsed with laughter and shock. Yes, I suppose it took about ten minutes for the shock to wear off. We were quite alone. Quite alone with 8,000 old tailors' dummies. That's what it amounted to. The message was clear and bold. All this just to remind you, just to remind you. To we who think we are going to live forever on this earth, this is just to remind you. All the greed, hate, love, graft, lust, strife, truth and lies, all the worldly goods, the insurance policies, the stocks and shares, the gold and silver. All these things have they suffered, enjoyed and possessed. And they are all hung up on the wall. Bang, just like that!

I know that's been said a million times before, there is nothing new to be said about man's allotted span and his ultimate demise. Nothing new at all, but I have never had it presented to me in such a devastating fashion. A tombstone by comparison says nothing. Uncle Charlie in his top hat and frock coat and grey cotton gloves leaning up against the wall there smiling at us says a lot. 8,000 Uncle Charlies say everything.

'You know, I don't feel very well.'

'No, a bit sick.'

'Yes, let's get out, I don't want to know any more.'

'Neither do I.'

'Come on, no not that way.'

'Yes it is.'

'No it isn't.'

'I could have sworn we came down there.'

'No it's up there, all the clergymen are up there surely, aren't they?'

'I don't know.'

Oh no, we can't get lost down here! Oh but we could, and did, but not for long and did they all chortle at us running around the caves, until at last—thank goodness—there are the stone steps! We scamper up them and out into the street.

That's nearly the end of the film. There's the cab driver with the droopy eyelid sitting motionless in the driver's seat with his head on one side.

'Oh dear, Tubby, he looks just like one of them.'

'Yes well, he comes here every day I expect.'

139

'Must be catching.'

'Bound to be.' We get in the cab and trot along the antique streets of Palermo, clip-clop clip-clop. And that's the end of the film.

CHAPTER TWELVE

A New York Perspective

One thing about life in New York—it's never dull for a minute, providing you are not on your own. To be alone anywhere for any length of time is of course pretty miserable, but to be alone in New York is absolutely horrible. Well, that was my experience. I almost used to dread waking up in the morning. But it's entirely different when you are with people you know and like and generally get on with. Then this fantastic city is a different place altogether to me.

I mean, even this old Scarsby Hotel is tolerable. By New York standards the Scarsby Hotel is pretty big and pretty old and it's reached a point in its life, I should say, where someone's either got to pull it together or pull it down. Well, if you leave a skyscraper to look after itself for too long it starts to age and decay, and the decay starts almost unnoticed where it can't be diagnosed, on the inside. That's what's happening to the Scarsby.

Well, we've got door trouble. The old door lock has tumbled and clicked for so long it's almost worn out. It's too tired to obey the brutal demands of the stern steel key. And so you have to fiddle the key carefully in the lock like a burglar with a wire feeling gently, trying to sense the exact place to flip the key over. Wait a bit that's it, no wait—ah, ah—that's it! We were lucky that time, for it can take up to ten minutes before you can persuade the tumblers to tumble. Still, that's not much to put right, is it? One door lock. Ah yes, but all the door locks were put in at the same time and they've all worn out together and there're hundreds and hundreds of them. Every corridor you walk down in the

Scarsby you'll find three or four crouching, cursing, amateur burglars doing a bit of breaking and entering.

And as I stand at the bedroom window on the fifteenth floor looking out at that gigantic cemetery of skyscrapers I can't help wondering what sort of shape they're all in. But at the moment the Scarsby provides everything we need and lots of things we don't need. Not really. Well, every room has a television set and a radio. Yes, every room. A television set in a bedroom is as important as a bed. It's an interesting set made of tin. A stout tin casing artistically grained to look like wood. But it works quite well. I always switch it on the moment I get out of bed in the morning and I switch on the radio as well. Not that I can pretend to pay attention to both, but they make such a racket that they're sure to wake up Tubby Foster.

He is rather a heavy sleeper and it's always interesting to watch him react in his sleep to the voice, to that extraordinary radio voice: 'We bring you the news every hour on the hour. It is seven o'clock and the temperature this morning in balmy downtown Manhattan is 63, the humidity 66, the air pollution is down to five and the pollen count by courtesy of the Jewish hospital Long Island, is one.'

Tubby Foster lifts his heavy lids. 'What's the pollen count?'

'Just one, by courtesy of the Jewish Hospital, Long Island.'

'They're not trying out there.'

No, I don't think they are. They sent out that short-sighted pollen counter again this morning—the one with the thick glasses. He can't count pollen for pussy, same old story every morning.

I expect they say to him: 'Right, how many pollens did you count this morning, then?'

'Just one.'

'*Just one*? Look, yesterday it was one, it was one the day before that and the day before that. Last week you even came back twice with no pollen count at all! The count of the pollens was nil—down to *zero*! Look, do us a favour will you, will you find some more pollens to count otherwise we got nothing to be courteous about any more? All the sneezers will be out of business, what's going to happen to all the dope we carry for hay fever? Look, couldn't you sneak up on a daisy or sumpin' and belt the hell out of it so we get some pollen for once? Hey, what do you say, okay? Okay.'

'No, the pollen count is really in a bad way,' I say.

'Certainly is. What's the air pollution this morning?' Tubby asks.

'That's down to five, I'm afraid.'

'Mmm, we'll soon put that right.' And Tubby Foster lights his first cigarette of the day and sits in bed like an old railway engine, blowing at the signals.

'You know that smoking in bed carries a fine of fifty dollars, don't you?'

'Yes.'

'You'll finish up in Alcatraz, you know that don't you?'

'Yes.'

'You ought to be ashamed of yourself you know, it's only crooks and the Mafia that smoke in bed, that's why there's a fine of fifty dollars for this despicable offence, I've a good mind to call the cops.' Here they come: *Waaaawaaawaaawaaa* whoop whoop *waaawaaa.* Yes, there go the cats and the gibbons, the police and the fire brigade. That's what they sound like—cats and gibbons.

'They have probably had a tip-off about some heel smoking a pipe in bed on Park Avenue, so watch it!'

'Yes,' agrees Tubby. 'I say, look at that!'

'Hey, what? That television?' Oh yes, that *is* good. Bright and early in the morning and there's an advertisement for salt. I can see it quite clearly in the bathroom mirror as I shave.

Now how would you advertise salt? Yes, salt, ordinary table salt that you shake over your food. Well, you can only say that it's saltier I suppose, or that it makes a man of you, or that women prefer men who wallop their chips with salt. No, that won't do. Old hat.

This ad is scathingly scientific, and they have slow-motion highly-magnified film to prove it. Well, did you know that salt bounces? Yes, it bounces. Scientific tests have conclu-

sively proved that salt bounces. Look here's the film to prove
it coming up now. Someone shakes a salt sifter over a plate of
T-bone steak and French fries. Well, of course you can see
it's quite useless. Under the microscope you can see that the
grains of salt fall just like big hailstones, a few of them land
on your steak and French fries but look at all the rest, they
are bouncing on the plate, up and down and clean off the
table. They do it again. Yes, it's fantastic. Over three-
quarters of the salt you shake out in your life bounces where
you don't want it. What do you think of that? Straight off
your plate, all over the floor, under the piano, into your
turnups, all into the dog's dinner, I mean, it's *disgusting*.

'What would your neighbours think, Tubby, if they knew
that not only did you smoke in bed, but that your dining
room was full of salt all bouncing about?'

'I'd never be able to face them again.'

'Exactly.'

And here comes the new scientifically-prepared, non-
bouncing salt. Look at that! One squirt from the old sifter
and, *splat*, the lot is right in the middle of the T-bone steak,
splat, another bull's eye on the French fries. It's brilliant!
You see—not one particle of that salt bounced. I don't know
how they do it, but it's nice to know that soon we'll be able to
live a life free from the bouncing salt.

No doubt other things will soon come to light. Perhaps
they'll invent a non-creeping marmalade. I mean, I've
known marmalade creep from a piece of toast right around
the back of my neck without me knowing it. And I think it's
high time we had a non-wander chocolate. All chocolate is
terribly nomadic, especially in the summer in a motor car.
I've known plain chocolate wander from the glove compart-
ment right around to the spare wheel on a warm day.

Still, we must get on: what's the time? It is eight o'clock
and the temperature in balmy downtown Manhattan is 63,
the air pollution is down to five and the pollen count by
courtesy of the Jewish Hospital, Long Island is one.

Right, this is just the morning to do a little aerial
photography. Yes, you can do that easily in New York.
Come on, it's a beautiful morning and our skyscraper hotel

is singing. It's always singing, this big sad building, singing its melancholic mechanical musical heart out, *scoobiedoobiedobedobedobe*. Along the corridors and down the lifts, *scoobiedoobiedobedo*, into the lobby and down to the restaurant, *scoobiedoobiedo*, and as we wait for the taxi on the side walk I can hear it singing like a great beehive with a thousand tidy cells and one big singing bee, *scoobiedoobiedo*.

Here's a cab. Now this morning we have arranged to do something that anyone with ten dollars can do as easily as anything. Take a cab to that towering tombstone in Park Avenue and book yourself a ride in a helicopter that takes off from the roof and twirls to Kennedy Airport.

Now there's no messing about in this skyscraper. It's in fine shape. It's incredibly efficient. 22,000 people come to work every day in this one building alone, and they've all got to be sorted and slithered into their little compartments by nine o'clock and then unsorted and slithered out again at five. So you can't mess about. The entrances are big and glassy, the lifts slip up and down like bubbles in gently simmering water. It's pretty well the last word in modern, clean-cut, forward-thinking, progressive architecture.

And for a single gigantic building where 22,000 people work and eat it is remarkably inoffensive. That sounds like a rotten compliment really, but it isn't. Well, take the new skyscrapers that they've built on Sixth Avenue, all black glass and shining steel. Exciting? Yes. Dramatic? Yes. Sensational? Yes. Beautiful? Ah, well, *now* you're talking. I can't define beauty. All I can say is that without it all those exciting dramatic sensational qualities either become boring, or else they drive you mad. That's why life is generally less worrying and easier with inoffensive buildings.

But of course this morning this particular skyscraper is exciting as well. Just imagine strolling into the entrance hall, ambling over to the counter in the corner and asking for two tickets for the helicopter that takes off from the roof.

'Yes sir, your flight will be called in about ten minutes. Would you go to the waiting lounge on the fifty-seventh floor?'

You really feel that you are living in the space age. All

those Jeff Hawke strip cartoons are gradually coming true. We step into a glorious metal bubble and go simmering up and up and up and burst gently on the surface of floor 57, the waiting lounge.

We can't believe it! The waiting lounge is a perfect reproduction of the interior of an olde worlde English country pub. Gorblimey! Well, there's nothing else you can say for a second. There's the old familiar scene: solid oak windsor wheel-back chairs, splendid oak seventeenth-century tables, great beefy Elizabethan court cupboards, copper warming pans.

I don't know whether to roll about laughing, or burst into tears. Well, it's the shock you see. I mean, one minute I'm in a make-believe space-age world, surging skywards in an express lift, and the next I'm smashed back into the jolly rollocking doublet-and-hose world of Good Queen Bess. There's nothing wrong with either world but bunging them both together, *bonk*, just like that, is such a poignant reminder of our general discontent, that we are never at the right place at the right time, that we really don't like being where we are now and we like to think we are somewhere else, back in the past or away in the future. Still, it's very nice to sit and wait in a comfortable oak windsor chair, way up almost in the clouds.

But we don't have to wait very long, a smart young lady comes over to us and says, 'Would you care to go on up now, please? The helicopter will be arriving in a few minutes.'

She points to a shining, chromium escalator that sneaks up behind an Elizabethan court cupboard. I must say I hadn't noticed it there before. We say farewell to the world of Elizabeth and the Tavern: And so good gentles all, we make our fond goodbyes, for we go hence to hover in the skies.

And we glide up to the roof. No helicopter in sight yet. Now, I don't know if you've ever watched someone start to build a house, but if you look at the foundations at the beginning of the operation they seem minute. I mean, that *tiny* little square of concrete, you'll never get a whole house on that, not with a kitchen and lounge and dining room and everything, oh no, *never*, in there? You need to make it oooh, at least *three* times the size . . . Well, that's what it seems like. This roof up here seems like that. It's tiny. We've been in the building underneath, I know, and it's enormous, but I can't help that, the roof's tiny. You'll never get a helicopter on that!

We wait in a little penthouse at the end of the roof, and there's a very friendly helicopter-landing controller waiting with us.

'Won't keep you a couple of minutes, it's due in now.'

'How big is this helicopter?'

'Oh, it's big.'

'How many people does it carry?'

'Oh, twenty-five.'

'Twenty-five, that's big all right. And it lands on that little roof out there?'

'Yes sir, right on that little roof out there, at the end of the blue carpet.'

'Oh, I see.' There's a strip of blue carpet running from the penthouse across to the middle of the roof. It's a beautiful carpet, not a wrinkle in it anywhere.

'How do you keep the carpet so flat?'

'It's stuck down.'

'Oh, you can't take it up when it rains?'

'Hell no.'

'So it's out there in the sopping rain and in the scorching heat?'

'Right.'

'Marvellous carpet.'

'Right.'

'How long does it last?'

'Oh, I don't know exactly. Three or four months maybe.'

'Then what happens to it?'

'We rip it up.'

'And put fresh down?'

'Right.'

'Expensive pastime, isn't it?'

'Hell no, we don't have to pay for it. The manufacturers of the carpet put it down for an advertisement.'

'Oh I see.'

'Know what? They wanted to carpet the whole area.'

'What, the whole roof?'

'Yeah, they figured it would be a swell advertisement if they put carpet down over the whole area.'

'Why didn't they?'

'Well, this is classified as an airport and any alterations or additions to the runways or landing areas have to be notified to the proper authorities.'

'Ah, and the authorities didn't like the idea?'

'Hell no, they thought it was great but they wouldn't allow it. Well, they figured it this way: no airport in the whole of the United States is carpeted, and so-what-the-hell, they didn't see why they should be the first to give permission to have an airport carpeted.'

'Ah, playing safe, eh?'

'Right. They thought that everybody would want their airports carpeted.'

Well, I don't know. Must say, it would brighten up London Airport no end to drop down through the fog on to twenty acres of the best bright red Axminster, and the Persians would make a smashing job of Teheran Airport with some of their flowery carpets . . .

Okay, here it is. It must have come up from behind us because I didn't see it, but there it is: a tremendous helicopter settling down on the roof in front of us. There's plenty of room for it. The two sets of choppers are flailing about. I must say it's a nasty, angry-looking machine. It looks half-barmy, like a hornet that can't find its way home, and now that they've opened the door of the penthouse we can hear those crazy choppers slashing the air—*phewphew-phewphew*.

The passengers from Kennedy Airport disembark and come ducking down the carpet, but there's no need for them to duck at all, the choppers chop away several feet above their heads. Now it's our turn to go aboard. And we walk slowly down the only blue-carpeted airport in the world— *tewetewtewtewtewyah*—it's no good, you've got to duck, it's impossible not to, those choppers force you into the ground and we practically climb into the helicopter on our knees.

But we get aboard all right. A charming hostess closes the door and the threshing hornet lifts itself a few feet off the roof and it just hangs there with its arms gesticulating as though it doesn't know what the dickens to do next. Well, that's what it feels like. And then it edges slowly backwards like an uncertain horse being forced back into the shafts of a cart. It is quite the most terrifying sensation I have ever experienced because we are now hanging over the street. It's like one of those frantic Harold Lloyd films. The front wheels of the helicopter are just resting on the parapet of the building and the body of the machine is hanging, just waggling helplessly over the street. And we are sitting in the tail. There's that nightmare shot of the street hundreds and hundreds of feet below, little beetle motor cars and tiny pin-head people.

The helicopter is like that character in a comic cartoon who is being chased over a cliff, he keeps on running in thin air before he sees there's no ground underneath him anymore and then he goes *doooooh*! and plummets into the terrible void. That's just what's going to happen to us, *doooooh*! No, this weird animal suddenly whistles up a tremendous power from somewhere and surges up, banks right then left, and then it slashes off, carving a great arc around Manhattan.

If ever you are in New York, and you have ten dollars to spare, take my advice and try this. I know it scares the pants off you for a few seconds but it's terrific. Look, we are flying around the Empire State Building, flying up among the skyscrapers. This is the twentieth century all right.

Of course, we've got to have skyscrapers, they are magnificent things. They really are incredible monuments to our skill, ingenuity and stubborn will to live. You don't feel this until you fly about amongst them. Well, up here you are on an equal footing you see. The reason why I've been saying all those horrible things about skyscrapers is because I've always viewed them from street level, and at street level skyscrapers obviously make you feel diminutive, measly, insignificant. Who do they think they are? The blinking great bullies towering up there, making us crawl around them like little ants. Of course, you've got to be horrible to

149

them in self defence. But up here it's just the opposite.

Oh pity, we're striking off now, away from Manhattan towards Kennedy Airport, and quite suddenly the concrete giants begin to shrink, down, down they go from eighty storeys to thirty to ten to two to one, to nothing less than nothing, because now we are chopping low over a tremendous cemetery.

It's extraordinary, I really thought those tombstones were buildings for a moment, and there must be thousands and thousands of them tucked away down there. I don't think that any air company could have arranged a more dramatic flight, a flight so full of the most obvious symbolism. Purely accidental of course, but in a couple of minutes they drag right before your very eyes the pageant of man from his towering marble pinnacle to his lowly stone slab. Very impressive, very impressive.

We spend a few minutes at Kennedy Airport and catch the next helicopter back. Here we go again, the pageant of man, but this time in reverse. The tombstones, the low buildings growing slowly up and up and finally shooting up around us. There's our tiny roof down there with the blue finger of carpet pointing to where we ought to land. It looks impossible but we slowly dingle, dangle, slither, slide and drop gently right beside the blue carpet.

'Have a good trip?'

'It was wonderful!'

'Good, have fun!'

'Thanks, and have fun yourself.'

Down the chromium escalator, back into Jolly Jack Falstaff's favourite tavern. And so, kind gentles all, yet since this day began, we've travelled swift as light through man's allotted span. And now get we hence out of this Tudor tearoom into our metal orb that falls like a cooling bubble to the street.

'Well, that's a wonderful way to start a day.'

'Now what shall we do?' Tubby asks.

'Well, there are dozens of things to do in New York. There's Central Park—that's pretty good. And there are all those museums up around Central Park.'

150

'Still, it's a pity to go inside on a lovely day like this.'

'Well, we can take a boat out to the Statue of Liberty or a boat around Manhattan Island, that ought to be good, don't forget we ought to have fun.'

'Oh yes, we ought to have fun.'

'Well, what do you think?'

It was then that I saw it, in a shop on Fifth Avenue. It was a large brass spinning top. An eight-sided brass spinning top. You remember that old game we all used to play called 'Put and Take'? Well, this is like a Put and Take top, only instead of having 'Put 2' 'Take all' and so on written on it, this top simply has 'Yes' and 'No' engraved alternately on each side. And the ticket underneath it says that it is a decision maker. *A decision maker*! Yes, I get it—if you have a decision to make you simply spin the top and whichever side lands face up, yes or no, then there's your decision for you. Barmy! And yet it isn't, you know. The longer we stare at the decision maker in the window the more logical it becomes. I mean, there are times when the old noodle gets addled and can't even decide whether to have another drink or not. That's when you spin your decision maker and hope it comes up 'Yes'. If you think about it there are hundreds of decisions to make every day and half of them you leave floating about in abeyance, like: Shall I phone so and so, yes or no? *Spin*. No. Good. Shall I skip lunch and just have a sandwich? *Spin*. Yes. Bother.

Well, at least it is being positive. And in America you must be positive. Wonder if the President's got one? Let's buy one. We go in.

'Good day, gentlemen.'

'A decision maker, please.'

'Surely. You two gentlemen want one each?'

'No, just one between the two, we aren't as undecided as all that.'

'Exactly.'

'Er, do many people buy decision makers?'

'Oh why, yes, we sell a lot of decision makers.'

'Good, it's nice to know that there are lots of people about who don't know which way to turn.'

'Yes.'

'Well, thank you very much, goodbye.'

'Goodbye, sir, come back.'

'Why, what's the matter?'

'Nothing sir.'

'But you said "Come back." '

'Yeah, I meant come back again sometime.'

'Oh, I see.' Difficult to get used to that—come back. It sounds to be such an order like, have fun. Sometimes you get them both together after you've bought something in a store . . . 'Well, thank you, goodbye.' 'Goodbye, now, come back. Hey. Have fun . . .'

'Right, now what are we going to decide with our decision maker?'

'We're going to decide where to go, Tubby.'

'Oh, yes, right.'

'Well, shall we go up to Harlem?' We spin the decision maker, it turns up no. 'Well, shall we go over to the Bowery?' We spin it again. No. 'Well, shall we go out to the Statue of Liberty?' Yes.

'Well, that's it then, seems to work very well doesn't it, the decision maker?' Yes, I'm very pleased with it. I think this year's model gives better decisions than last year's. No doubt about it.

We set off to take a boat to the Statue of Liberty and in a couple of minutes we are at the waterfront, the old Battery, where there's a boat waiting to take trippers out to the Statue. And we go aboard.

This is something else that you must do in New York, visit the Statue of Liberty. It was a gift from the people of France to the people of the United States. The sculptor was M. Bartholdi, the engineer was M. Eiffel—oh, but there's one thing that I mean to find out about the statue, it's worried me for years.

'Er, excuse me, can we go up inside?'

'Sure, take the elevator to the tenth floor and then the spiral stairway.'

It's quite an experience climbing the spiral stairway. Well, the statue is absolutely hollow, it's made of sheets of copper hammered around a steel skeleton. Up we go, around and around, until we reach the great copper dome head. And we look out through the crown of Liberty across the water to Manhattan. When I say that it's a heady experience, I'm not trying to be funny. Here we are in this great copper head, three hundred feet above the sea, and look, here comes a helicopter buzzing around our heads, that's something else we must do, I'm all for these helicopter trips . . . *Beee*, who's that? I'd know that voice anywhere of course, it's the *Queen Elizabeth*. There she sails in the sun for England, and we're watching her go home from the crown of the Statue of Liberty.

And I suppose we had better make our way back to our temporary home. When we get back to our skyscraper hotel, that evening, it's still singing itself sadly to sleep, *scoobiedoobiedobedobedobe, scoobiedoobiedobedodobe*. And next morning we have the voice again.

'We bring you the news on the hour, every hour. The temperature in balmy downtown Manhattan is 63, the air pollution is down to five and the pollen count by courtesy of the Jewish Hospital, Long Island is one.'

'He's still not trying.'

'No, he's dead scared to kick that daisy around.'

'Well, what do we do today, Tubby?' I spin the decision maker. It says yes. Right, that's what we do today then. Yes. Yes, that's what we do today. Yes. That's the great thing about America, it is positive. Yes. It's very positive. Yes.

CHAPTER THIRTEEN

Nashville, Tennessee—the Real America

There's nothing like a touch of curiosity to keep you going and in America, of course, your curiosity is not only aroused, it's fully woken up and slapped in the face and dragged out of bed. But the one part of the anatomy that slowly ceases to be at all curious about anything in America is the tongue. Those eccentric, delicate, expectant taste buds just shrivel and refuse to flower, like spring blooms in frosty weather. America just hasn't the right sort of climate for taste buds—in fact, I rather suspect that they are regarded as a goddam nuisance.

Well, they interfere with the automated food intake stations, do taste buds. I mean, why complicate a simple food intake pattern of starch, carbohydrates, protein and vitamins by allowing taste buds to reject out of hand, or rather, out of mouth, a perfectly balanced wedge of cotton wool and plastic mince and gravy? Can't have that sort of thing going on. Whatever next?

I suppose that breakfast was about the best meal of the day. It was always the same but it was bearable. You sit on a stool at a counter. The gentleman breakfast dispenser usually wears a natty little cheesecutter cap and a white coat. It's not a bit of use being pleasant and chatty and saying, ah, now let me see, I wonder if it would be at all possible for you to sort of fry my eggs on both sides? Could you do that? You know, not too much, sort of lightly done so that they do not exactly solidify, but still retain that rather pleasant, uncertain quality . . . ?

If you do say that, the breakfast dispenser will treat you to a glare that burns with enough contempt to melt a hole in a knickerbocker glory. The fact is, he doesn't understand what the heck you are blabbering about. It's interesting, because we are both supposed to speak English. But he doesn't get it. He will start from the beginning.

'You want bacon? Okay?'

'Yes.'

'You want eggs? Okay?'

'Yes.'

'How do you want them?'

'Well, I rather thought that if you could . . .'

'Look, do you want 'em sunny-side up, or over easy?'

'Ah yes, I see.' And after a little experimentation you find the correct code for ordering. In other words you are dealing with a computer and you have to feed it the abbreviated language it understands.

It's reasonable, of course, but it turns breakfast time into a sad affair when you are reminded every morning that the elaborate tapestry of words that we have woven for ourselves through the centuries can be so ruthlessly unpicked, to leave us with the threadbare warp and weft of what do you want? how much? hello and goodbye. Of course, if you're not the talkative sort at breakfast, it's fine. When the breakfast dispenser approaches you for your order, you've got it all ready.

'Good day, gentlemen. Alrightee, tomato juice?'

'Tomato juice.'

'Bacon and egg?'

'Bacon and egg.'

'Eggs over easy?'

'Eggs over easy.'

'Coffee?'

'Coffee.'

And you get your complete breakfast on one plate. I must say, it takes a bit of getting used to. There is no room in the organisation for side plates. No sir, no side plates and only one knife. There's your breakfast bacon, two eggs over easy on the south side of the big plate. On the north side, on the perimeter, lies a wrapped pat of butter, a tiny gobbet of plastic potted jam and a wrapped bread roll. Well, it isn't bread, it's a sort of cotton wool. Your one knife and fork and spoon are presented in an envelope. Well, of course, it's like an awkward picnic. You crack your roll open on the counter and it scatters flaky brown crumbs everywhere. You try to butter it with an eggy knife and get butter all over your bacon. The jam naturally crawls everywhere looking for a side plate. The mess you leave behind really looks like a monkey house.

The one consoling thing about breakfast is, of course, that you have your own personalised juke box in front of you on the counter. Nice thought, isn't it? An affair the size of a biscuit tin. And there is one for each customer. These juke boxes are put in front of everybody to make sure there is no talking. You get stuck into your sunny-side up, or your over easy, and choose your tune from a list. Drop a nickel in the biscuit box, dial the number you want and it comes from some master-juker in the basement *scoobiedoobedo*. I must say that *scoobiedoobiedoo* is about the most popular tune to have for breakfast. Lots of people choose it. It does relieve the monotony a bit.

But just lately our taste buds have been blooming quite nicely. Well, here in St Louis, Missouri, the flavours are coming back. The feeding automatons are not in control. Real people are actually smoking hams, savouring soups and spicing cakes. The smells that float away from the kitchens are good homely smells. We have just had a fine flavoured meal aboard the *River Queen*, on the great Mississippi river. The *River Queen* is a beautiful Mississippi river paddle-boat. You know the sort, like a tremendous houseboat, with a long cylinder paddle at the back and a couple of tall, gay chimneys. Once it was the thing to do, to take a trip on a pleasure steamer like this, up and down the Mississippi river. You could be away for weeks, living in luxury, with the scenery slowly changing all around you all day long.

The present *River Queen* was built in the '20s—a perfect replica of an old nineteenth-century river boat. They have copied the fixtures, fittings and furniture, and it's all been there long enough to take on the elegant atmosphere of those

156

spacious days. It's very convincing. But it is now just a restaurant moored in the middle of St Louis on the Mississippi river. Every now and again the *River Queen* really goes to work and splashes up and down the Mississippi for one of the great film companies. She had quite a big part in *Gone with the Wind*. But apart from the occasional bit of freelance acting, she slops peacefully in the wash of the modern diesel barges that slide about this great waterway.

St Louis, I suppose, has the widest streets of any city in the world. They are so wide and so long that people are just lost in them and the place seems deserted. I have never known a place so big and so mysteriously empty. Of course we spent quite a lot of time looking up in the sky and so we could have missed some of the passing population. Well, we were looking up at this arch they've built. This arch? Yes, that's exactly what we said, this arch. Well, they wanted one, and why shouldn't they? You can have anything if you're prepared to pay for it, and this arch is costing *millions*.

To start with, they tore down eleven acres of buildings beside the Mississippi river. That's the place to put the arch in, you see. And then they put it in. Took them quite a long time. Well, it's quite a lot of arch and it's plated with stainless steel. It is the size and shape of a rainbow. Yes, a rainbow. A rainbow rather pointed at the top like the bow of a ship. It is enormous—over 600 feet high. And this is the strange thing about it: as I said, it is plated with stainless steel, so that it reflects, or rather takes on, the colour of the sky around. On a grey day, it's grey. When the sky is blue, it's blue, and it goes pink in the sunset, so you are never quite sure that it's there. And yet you can see it, can't you? Yes, no, it's gone again, no, there it is! A great ghostly rainbow. A tremendous presence. That's what it is—a presence.

Now this is something that a building does not usually achieve: the effect of making you feel horribly aware of it, when you are not even looking at it. The St Louis arch does this. Whenever you are in the city, you have to keep looking over your shoulder, like walking the lonely road at twilight; yes, it's there.

When we first saw it, we went as close as we could to it. It wasn't quite finished then and it was fenced off and we agreed that it was about the biggest monument to nothing that we had ever seen. It is supposed to represent the gateway to the West, which is a bit confusing, because if you're coming from the other way it's the exit to the East, but nobody mentions that. But it certainly doesn't look like the gateway to the West, it looks more like International Croquet Week or the National Steelbenders Convention, or if you must have a name for it, all that goes up, must come down. In the short time we were in St Louis we grew very fond of this ghostly rainbow. Soon the elevators will be working and the tourists will be able to travel inside this great rainbow and view the Mississippi and St Louis city in real comfort.

We would like to have stayed in St Louis a lot longer. Well, we were enjoying our flavours again and we were enjoying the ebony giggly girls that served them. The one that served our lunch yesterday was practically hysterical with laughter. I don't know what was so funny about us. Every time she approaches our table, she just folds over with laughter.

'Ahahahahaha, which one of you handsome gentlemen is having the steak? Hahahahaha, glory.'

'Well, I am, actually, and what's so funny about it? Why are you laughing so?'

'Glory, I'se laughing outside but I'se crying inside.'

That's it, laughing outside, crying inside. 'All right then, what are you crying about?'

'I'se so tired.'

'Tired?'

'Yeah, glory I'se so tired! I done started working here ten o'clock this morning and these trays is so heavy, glory, hahahaha.'

'What time do you finish?'

'Three o'clock.'

'Oh well, that's not too bad.'

'Glory, these trays is so heavy! I'se so tired, at three o'clock I'se going right back home to my pappy, yessir hahahaha.'

'Back home to your pappy?'

'Yessir, hahahahaha.'

It's no good, she can't help laughing. Every time she passes our table—hahahaha, glory, haha—laughing outside, crying inside, and moving about the hot restaurant like a badly-manipulated string puppet, her skinny arms and legs not quite under control. At three o'clock she's going back home to her pappy, and just after three o'clock we flew away from St Louis to Nashville, Tennessee.

Now there's nothing remarkable about Nashville, Tennessee. We thought that we'd just stop there for a night and drive to the Smoky Mountains before returning to New York. We did not know that Nashville was a great recording centre. Yes, a place where they make records of all the tortured noises that they call singing nowadays. We also did not know that at Nashville they broadcast a famous weekly radio programme called Grand Ole Opry, and that this programme has been running for forty-one years. *Forty-one years!* So you see, quite a lot goes on in Nashville.

One other very important thing that we did not know was that on the very day we arrived in Nashville they were holding a disc jockey convention. No, I'm not joking. We walked right into the middle of it. A disc jockeys' convention and there were 2,500 of them. Yes, I'll repeat that: 2,500 disc jockeys all in a heap. I suppose you can count the number of disc jockeys we have in this country on your fingers—give or take a digit. So you get a pretty good idea of the state of American radio as a whole, when you realise that there are 2,500 disc jockeys who can be spared to come to this convention, and they are all here in Nashville today. All the boys that sport all the qualifications that go to make disc jockeys: the show-offs, the jokers, the smooth, the smiling, the relaxed, the confident, the vital, the dynamic, the homely, the friendly, the brisk, the bright, the whispery, the shouty, they are all here with their agents, managers, wives, employers, microphones, records and amplifiers. It is a rattling collection of tin cans in gold lamé suits, white suede bootees and six-gallon hats and electric guitars. Walking into this lot is just like walking into a mad sort of nightmare.

It started when we arrived at a big hotel in Nashville. We

had driven there from the airport in a big slob hired automobile. Music was yawling from a battery of loud-speakers on the corner of the street. Music? Well, I found out later that it's known as Country and Western style, and it's very popular hereabouts, and basically all of it sounds to me like this: *tararararar*—I won't go on. A little of it goes a long way, right around the world I'm sorry to say.

Well, we unload our gear into the lobby of this very big hotel. Flashbulbs are splashing about all over the place. Smart men in white suede cowboy outfits are posing convincingly for the publicity and press men. Cute little dolls spoofed up as cowgirls, showing the leg well above the garter mark and giving the old cheesecake to kind friends one and all, and everybody's wearing a great green badge on his lapel. Badge? Well, really it's a plaque. It's as big as a plaque and inscribed on it is the name, description and home town of the wearer. It's exactly like the registration plate on a motor car. The gentle art of introduction is no longer necessary. You shout unashamedly to the world that you are Gradwick Blotcher of Station WYKF of Twinkletown, wherever it is.

We stand half bemused in the middle of this effervescent circus.

'I say, Tubby, where's your registration plate?'

'I'd be ashamed to put it up with a name like Foster.'

'I know Morris would look dead ordinary. Did you see who that was just went by?'

'No, who?'

'Conway Twitty.'

'Is that a fact?'

'Yes.'

'Not THE Conway Twitty?'

'Yes.'

'I hate to tell you who I've just seen.'

'Who?'

'Well, wait a minute, I've got to be careful; Elmer Fudpucker.'

'I don't believe you!'

'It's true, that was his name, Elmer Fudpucker.'

160

I know people can't help their names, but a name can be very misleading when you wear it on your heart and it says Conway Twitty or Elmer Fudpucker. At heart you may not be a Twitty or a Fudpucker.

'Say, hiya fellers! How are you doing?'

Hey, what's that? Who have we got here? Ah yes, his registration plate says he is George Kretch. Well, that's reasonable enough, and he comes from Indiana. Hey hey, wait a minute, wait a minute. He's looking for our registration plates and can't find them. He's at a loss, he doesn't know what to do. It's terrible. He's on the point of banging me on the back and shrieking out: 'Well what do you know, how are you Johnny Morris, Bristol, England, ya son of a gun. How've ya bin?' But without my registration plate I'm just a little lump in a tweed hat.

'Say who are you? What company do you represent? Where are you from?'

'Well, the B.B.C. Bristol, England.'

'The goddam B.B.C., goddam Bristol, goddam England! Well come on in, the party's swinging. Come on in.'

He leads us to the doorway of an enormous ballroom.

'Say Jim, the goddam B.B.C., goddam Bristol, goddam England.'

'Hiya fellers, hiya.'

'Hiya.' There's no doubting the genuine friendliness of these disc jockeys.

'Say, what size hat do you wear?'

'Hat, hat, what size hat?'

'Yeah, what size hat?'

'Well, it's six and three-quarters or seven or something, why?'

'Okay, pardner, have fun!' He plonks a six-gallon cowboy hat on my head. He plonks a six-gallon cowboy hat on Tubby Foster's head. They really are very beautiful felt hats. The real thing. Off-white, take-it-easy, six-gallon hats.

'But these aren't our hats.'

'They are now. Go on, have fun.'

'Yeah, come on fellers.'

I must say that secretly I have always wanted to wear one

161

of these great six-galloners. And I must also say that a six-gallon hat is just about the biggest morale booster that a man can crown himself with. The easy confidence that blossoms inside you when you put on a rough-riding, off-white, six-gallon hat, is really astonishing. Look in the mirror there at the two of us. Phew, we look just like that sharp-shooting bunch from the Lazy Bar X ranch. Sure to be a heap of trouble when we come into town. We roll into the ballroom. It's an incredible sight. The ballroom isn't being used for dancing tonight. It's just one gigantic bar, and in it there are about three thousand disc jockeys, all wearing real felt off-white six-gallon hats. The air is blue with cigar smoke and the clamour is just like the monkey house when the monkeys have been upset. Everybody's standing up, those that can. There are a few chairs around the wall for those who have had a hard day. George Kretch drags us over to the counter.

'Hi, come on. Scotch on the rocks for everyone!'

Scotch on the rocks! 'Look let me do this.'

'Aw, shut up, it's all free, all free, it's all on the Cacaphone Recording Company.'

All free on the Cacaphone Recording Company! Phew, no wonder everyone's so free and easy.

'Okay fellers, mud in your eye, good luck to the Cacophone records.'

George Kretch hands us all a tremendous measure of best scotch whisky in paper cups. He notices the slight dismay on my face. What's the matter, don't you like scotch? Oh yes, yes I like it very much. I was thinking, quite honestly, of all those canny master magicians of Speyside who distill this precious water of life with such loving care. If only they knew.

'Okay. Bottoms up fellers!' George Kretch empties his paper cup down his throat. Wow! and hands it back to the bartender. 'Okay, fill 'em up again, come on, come on fellers, we're having a ball with the Cacaphone Recording Company.'

In the hard and crafty drinking world, George Kretch is what is known as a front runner. He sets a tremendous pace.

We follow him as best we can for several laps but we're not fast enough for him and we lose sight of him. When he disappeared I had two paper cups full to the brim, one in each hand and I was talking to a six-foot-three cowboy in a gold lamé suit. He was holding up a cowgirl whom he said was pretty tired. Her head kept flopping forward and her hat wouldn't stay on. In fact, the law of gravity was beginning to assert itself all over. All sorts of stuff was falling down. The floor was littered with paper cups and cigar butts and six-gallon hats. And some of the six-gallon hats had still got cowboys in them. It was time to go. I remember picking my way through the mellow muddle and confusion and looking back through the thick blue smoke at all those nodding, wobbling, six-gallon hats.

We wore six-galloners next day in Nashville. Well, the other three thousand wore theirs, and we sank deep into our sponge car automobile, waved goodbye to all the other six-gallon hats, and drove out of town up into the Smoky Mountains. As mountains go, the Smoky Mountains don't go very high, which is a very fortunate thing because the trees grow all over them. Those wonderful magnificent trees. It's getting towards the end of October and they are still on fire. Red maple, silver maple, black maple, sugar maple, the mulberries, chestnuts, hickories, aspens all quivering, flickering and falling, showering sparks of colour into the tumbling, bubbling rivers. Settling soft and warm on the forest floor where the black bears scuffle and then come scrounging down to the wayside dustbins. Yes, we saw several black bears in the Smokies. They are smallish bears and not aggressive. They just like to be left alone and are quite happy as long as we leave them alone and keep the dustbins nicely topped up.

Yes, there are still some black bears left in the Smokies. There are still some Red Indians left there too. We saw our first one when we drove into Cherokee. We came around a sharp bend into the town and there he was on the corner, in his full astonishing regalia. A feathered head-dress was growing out of his magnificent head, trailing beautifully right down to the ground. The moment you see him, you say

163

it, you can't help it, you say 'How', and you stop the car and get out. That's what you are meant to do because he stands outside the trading post which is a souvenir shop.

We saw him later that day when he'd finished work, in a restaurant without his display kit, just wearing jeans and a shirt and eating a beefburger and beans. It was a sad picture. But he is one of the luckier ones, the luckier ones who supply the tourist with his souvenirs. The ones who are organised and trained to make moccasins and jackets and knives and bullwhips and traditional jewellery for sale at the trading posts. The unlucky ones are the ones who just can't cope, cannot change, and despair. The speed at which our civilisation has overtaken them has completely defeated them in more ways than one. Some of them manage a few months' work at Frontierland.

Frontierland is a few miles down the road from Cherokee and I suppose that you would call it an outdoor animated museum. It's quite astonishing. You drive up to a real High Noon sort of railroad station. You pay your money and you get aboard a real old Chattanooga-choo-choo. One of the original iron-horse engines with a cowcatcher and a *wheeo-wheeo* whistle and a clanging brass bell, *gongongonggong*. *Wheeoo*, here we go past an Indian village with wigwams and real Indians, and we get out five minutes later at a real old frontier town. There's a saloon, with real girls giving the old leg show, a jail, a sheriff's office, a bank, shops, a blacksmith's, a wheelwright's, a school, a church, a barber's shop, covered wagons, hitching rails, everything exactly as it used to be sixty or seventy years ago, and then every hour on the hour there's a gun fight. You get up on the stockade out of the way as the baddies ride into town. And then for five minutes, all hell is let loose. I must say, they do it very well. Shots come from everywhere. Chaps falling off balconies, out of windows, off horses, *crrkcrkcrrk*. Look at that fellow running for his horse, *crkcrkcrk*, got him! He does an agonised somersault and really bites the dust. And that's that.

Then you wander over to the Indian village. Amongst the teepees and the squaws and the braves they put on a pretty convincing ritual dance for you—*bobobobobobobaeooiaey bobobo-*

bobo. It's all extremely well done. It's all exactly as we've seen it on the films, and it's all sadly ironical to watch these Red Indians act out day after day, every hour, for our entertainment, a bit of the past that we took away from them, *bombombombom ieeayeieeay*.

And that is the end of the entertainment for today. Frontierland will be open again at nine o'clock tomorrow.

You can easily spend a whole day at Frontierland, looking at America as it used to be. Well that's very nice, because tomorrow we shall be seeing America as it is now once again. We are flying back to New York. That will be quite nice. And staying at that old Scarsby Hotel again. The big singing hotel, *scoobiedoobiedo*. That will be quite nice. And listening to the cats and gibbons again, *weeeeaaaweeeaaa whoos whoops weeeeaaweeeeaaaa*, well, that's not too bad. And then getting on that slashing helicopter and chopping around Manhattan to Kennedy Airport, now that will be nice. And then flying off across the Atlantic, back home. And that will be nice. Mmm, that will be *very* nice.

CHAPTER FOURTEEN

Muddling Through the French Countryside

It's quite incredible how sometimes you can create a dreadful muddle through no fault of your own. Tubby Foster and I seem to be quite good at it . . .

We had been driving for some hours when the petrol gauge said we needed petrol, so we pull into a garage and get out to stretch. The attendant sets the pumps whirring and I cast an eye over the car we are driving. It certainly has an arresting shape. It's just a shape, of course, but as you know the shape of things can persuade you to accept them or reject them. This car is totally acceptable—low to the ground with more than a touch of toughness.

I remember when we filled up in England before we came to France the young man at the garage said, 'That's a nice-looking car.'

'Yes.'

'I bet that won't half pull the birds.'

'Pull the birds?'

'Yes, pull the birds, cor, that car will pull the birds all right.'

I hadn't, quite honestly, thought of it like that. I'm past the age when I thought of a car as a bird-puller. In case you're not with me (and it took me some time to get with myself) a bird-puller is anything that is likely to attract the attention of young ladies. If you're six-foot-six, that pulls some birds. If you've got nice fair wavy hair, that pulls some birds. If you've got a twelve-bore shot gun and a couple of springer spaniels, a pipeful of the right tobacco and a glass of light ale, well, that pulls the birds too. If you've got all that

166

and a motor car like this one you're nothing but a dangerous magnet. Pull the birds? You've got to fight them off.

It's true I had noticed one or two birds turn and look at us as we passed through a small town. But then it's also true that one or two young men had shown some interest, but that could be because the car was British, and also because of its adventurous low shape. It was after we left Avignon that our car really attracted a lot of attention.

We spent a few nights in Avignon. There's much to see there, apart from the famous bridge. Although the bridge hasn't carried anyone across the river Rhone for more than 700 years—it was destroyed in 1226 by the King of France because the people of Avignon had made themselves into a republic and—would you believe it?—so big were they for their boots that they refused the King of France permission to pass through Avignon. He didn't like that and so he knocked their bridge down. Naturally. You must not be horrible to the King of France. Naturally. And the bridge has never been rebuilt.

But much of Avignon remains intact. It's a walled city and the battlements are in superb condition. They could even now delay a crusade for years. The old Pope's Palace still stands, for Avignon was the centre of Christendom when the Popes lived there in the fourteenth century. And there are restaurants there. But that goes without saying. Naturally. Oh, naturally.

Well, it was after we left Avignon that we came across this obstruction. We could see it from quite a distance and we knew that it was a fairly serious obstruction because the traffic in front was just skirting it on the wrong side of the road. But it seemed to be nothing but mud. Great lumps of grey-blue mud and dollops of gudge on our side of the road. Obviously a badly loaded site-clearing lorry had managed to drag itself out of a building bog somewhere, bang along here and leave a filthy trail for three or four hundred yards. Still, we'll scrub all around it. No, we can't; a big lorry suddenly presents itself, he's moving at us with a blind, relentless purpose the way that big bullying lorries do. We'll have to drive through the mud. Quick, shut the windows! Oh dear, our beautiful bird-pulling motor car. Gobble, gobble. It sounds like a ravenous pig at a trough—gobble, gobble. The mud thuds up under the mudguards and splatters underneath our lovely low car, but it hasn't much of a liquid consistency about it and it doesn't fly very high, it lies nice and low.

'The fellow that did that ought to be made to come and sweep it up.'

'Yes, he must have known he was making an awful mess.'

'Still, there's not a sign of him.'

'No, he's gone up there.'

Sure enough, the mud dwindles and does a right turn. Thank goodness we are rid of it.

We go on for a mile or two until we are stopped by the red traffic lights of a small town. Traffic lights are of course organised for stopping and starting motor cars, but strangely enough they often stop and start conversation that goes on in motor cars. I've often noticed it. We can be chatting away—hahaha, hohoho. Red light. Stop.

I realised we'd stopped chatting while we watched the red light and for the want of something to say and the fact that I hadn't asked him for a few days I said to Tubby, 'By the way, how's your old black tongue?'

'Much about the same, look.' He sticks his tongue out.

'Mmm, I don't think it's quite so black at the edges.'

'Don't you think so?'

'No, not quite. These traffic lights are taking a time, aren't they?'

'Yes, some of them do.'

It was then that I looked out of the wide window towards a greengrocer's shop. Two ladies with shopping baskets were staring at us with horror. Horror and the utmost disgust. Perhaps they'd seen Tubby's black tongue? They look as though they've seen Boris Karloff and Bella Lugosi doing a slow streak. It's quite unmistakable: one says to the other 'blleeeaaaah', the other mimes a short vomit as well 'ufffff', and they both belt off looking backwards at us.

'Well, we're not pulling the birds today.'

'No, I noticed that. Shall we stop for a glass of beer? I'm

feeling rather warm.'

'Well, we wound the windows up when we went through the mud.'

There's a café with a car park. We pull in and get out.

'You wouldn't know that we'd been through all that mud, hardly a splash on the—' Sniff, sniff. '—pooh. Something's died around here!' It's the most *awful* stench that ever stunk into a nostril. 'What on earth is it?'

'It's us,' says Tubby.

'Us?'

' 'Fraid so.'

Sniff, sniff. 'It is! It's the car!'

'Yes, lovely isn't it?'

'That mud wasn't mud, not to say *mud*,'

'No, not to say mud.'

It was the hundred years' deposit account of a well established and much respected cesspit. Something like that. And we've got it. Most of it at any rate. Stuck underneath our lovely low car. Not a hope of getting it out, wouldn't dream of even beginning—*poooo*. The exhaust's warmed it through a bit. Yes, the underneath of our car carries a six-inch layer of warm, active pong. We are the owners of a travelling stink bomb, a stink bomb weighing over a ton. Our beautiful bird-pulling car suddenly disgusts us. We walk away and leave it shimmering in a haze of stink.

As we walk towards the café a dog comes bounding out, *ow ow ow*. It's a black and dreadful-looking Doberman Pinscher, *ow ow ow*, one of those dogs that can never manage a well-tailored bark, they always sound as though they are choking with the sulphuric fumes of hell from whence they have just emerged, *ow ow ow*. You never know what to expect from *ow ow ow*. Very often the owner shouts out: 'He only wants to be friendly,' or, '*Ow ow ow*, don't run, stand still. Come here, Wolfgang!'

'I don't like the look of this one.'

'No, neither do I.'

Ow ow ow. He bounds right past us and gallops towards the car. He stops about a yard away from it and yowls at it—*ow ow ow*. Then gradually his yowling turns to a mournful howl, *ow ow ow yyoooowwwwyooow*, his tail drops, he slinks low and comes loping like a coward to the café, *yoooow*. He has recognised the smell of death, it seems. He cringes up to the waiter.

The waiter can't understand it. 'What's the matter with him, what's the matter with him?' and then the waiter's left nostril twitches, his head lifts like an antelope that senses something a bit dodgy. Sniff: 'Hey what is this, hey what is this?' He turns and looks at us with a mixture of indignation and suspicion on his face.

'Huh, pmpm tee tee,'—it's always best to take the initiative at times like this—'Huh, deux biers s'il vous plaît.'

Oui, deux bier. No need for both of us to say it. Oh no. He brings our beer and starts looking under the tables. At the back of the bar. It's the most uncomfortable beer we've had for a long time. He circles our table and then studies the Doberman Pinscher carefully.

'Let's go, shall we?'

'Yes, let's.' We leave him a very nice tip and make off towards our stink bomb. The waiter watches us from the doorway, a tea-cloth over his shoulder. It was then that our beautiful motor car let us down even further and very badly. Must have been nerves, but as we approached, it had a little accident, or as they say it forgot itself, went *gggrrgggr* and dropped a big dollop of cesspit from the rear mudguard on to the car park.

'Oh no,' *poooo*, 'quick, let's go.'

Oh, the shame that strikes the heart of every coward as he runs away. I saw them in the driving mirror as we roared out of the car park, the waiter and the Doberman Pinscher, both frozen with horror gazing at a stifling mess that might have been left by a passing dinosaur.

'What are we going to do about it?'

'I don't know, better try and find a car wash.'

'A car wash wouldn't be very happy with us, would it?'

'Still, we'll keep a look out for one.'

Yes, but it's like finding a policeman; we can't find a car wash and yet we seem to have seen the old *Lavage* notices up every few hundred yards. But not a sign. It's incredible how a silly accident like driving through the contents of a cesspit can overshadow your innocent life. Well, there was that incident at Les Baux. Les Baux is another of those wonderful surprises that Le France can serve up just like that. It's quite a sensational place, a settlement in pre-historic times. There are caves at the top of the limestone mountain at Les Baux. And then Les Baux became a fortress, a fortress that was virtually unassailable, it towers high on the top of a vertical cliff. Nothing could take it. Today there stands the old deserted city that hid in the fortress, the deserted cathedral where they prayed so confidently for deliverance. And at the top you can view without turning the head a thousand square miles of Provence.

'That was a fantastic place, wasn't it?'

'Yes, amazing.'

We were walking back to the car park at the bottom of the mountain. 'By jingo, Tubby, the air was strong up there wasn't it?'

'Yes, feel better for—oh lord!'

'What's the matter?'

'It's done it again.'

Oh, so it has, it's been very naughty, another great dollop in a car park. This is awful, it's like having an untrained puppy dog, you can't take it anywhere, well, you never know when it's going to let you down. It's strange the embarrassed panic that seizes everybody when a puppy 'misbehaves' itself. 'Oh look at that, damn the animal, get some ashes, water, keep the children away, rub his nose in it, put him in the garden quick, quick, quick!' It's true we do not wish to be associated with such things. We jump into the car. It's very sorry for what it's done, sensitive you see. Wants to run away, anywhere from what it knows now to be a big crime. It shoots in a confusion out of the car park, skids left down the hill.

'Hey, we're going the wrong way.'

'So we are, we'll turn around.' But we can't turn around for a mile or two until we find a gap and drive back past the car park. The attendant is there with a pole, a long pole, he's pushing something with the pole. I can't see what it is but the head is averted with a look of positive disgust.

But like Tubby's black tongue we learn to live with it.

'Care to do a television interview on the present situation?'

'Yes.'

'Mr Foster, not only have you a black tongue but you also have a disgusting smell about you all the time, don't you find this depressing?'

'Well, no, I've learnt to live with it actually.'

'But don't you find that people tend to reject you?'

'Well, maybe, but I accept that as a challenge.'

'Do you see any possibility of the situation easing?'

'At this point in time we must let nature take its course, the outcome of which could be made known sometime in the future.'

'Thank you for coming along.'

'Thank you.'

And that is just about the situation. Perhaps we've grown accustomed to the smell, perhaps we have really learned to live with it. But people do drift away from us whenever we stop at traffic lights or market squares. They leave us aloof and alone. Just a bit.

Yesterday, yesterday, we got rid of the smell! May I remind you, as if we shall ever forget, may I remind you that we had the misfortune to drive through the contents of a cesspit that had been spilled from a cesspit lorry on to the road. We couldn't avoid it and our low slung motor car got plastered underneath. Like a layer of ghastly pastry it stuck and hardened and oozed its terrible stench wherever we went. We couldn't get away from it, we couldn't lose it until it rained.

'Thank goodness for that, it's raining.'

'Yes, we are going to get a thunderstorm I think.'

'Yes, I think we are.' And it was a glorious thunderstorm, the best one I have ever known. It banged and flashed and the rain hammered and bouned off the road like grapeshot. It was a perfect pandemonium. Of course it took a little time to penetrate our underseal, but it did. *Grrrk*. There goes a lump. I saw it in the driving mirror sliding across the slippery road out of control. *Grrrcck.* I think we're getting rid of our embarrassment. Yes, it's started, it's like defrosting the fridge. You've got to be patient for a while and then it really begins falling away. *Grrk. Grrk.* I can't tell you the relief. The motor car knew too. It was a load off its mind. It gurgled through the rain and started purring like a pussy cat. *Brrrbrrrr.* And we swished through the beautiful body-cleaning water for a couple of hours until the rain dwindled, the clouds started to roll and tumble away, the road dried and the sun pushed through to say goodnight. Another half an hour and he would be gone.

'I suppose we had better think of finding somewhere to stay.'

'Suppose so. Well, here's a promising-looking town coming up. Let's stop and see what the book says about it.'

We find a space to park in the town square. 'Wonder if we're still smelling.'

'I wonder.'

We look around. People seem to be going about their business without concern. A group of men are chatting quite near to us.

'They don't seem worried, Johnny.'

'No, that's a change.'

Well, for the past couple of days people have just walked away from us, looking up in the sky, wondering. Puzzled, offended.

We get out: sniff, sniff.

'Smell anything?'

'No, it's gone.'

'I really think it has. Let's try at the back.' Sniff. Sniff. 'How's your side?'

'Sweet as a nut.'

'So's mine.'

'Good afternoon, something is wrong?' It's a policeman, a gendarme! Quite an advanced gendarme because he's neatly decorated with strips of gold here and there.

'You speak English, do you?'

'Naturally, I was in London for many years. But why are you smelling your motor car?'

173

That's a very good question: why are we smelling our motor car? Should be in the useful phrases book. Why are we smelling our motor car? It's a rotten question really, well, it demands such a long answer if you're going to be truthful. But he's a gendarme and he is naturally curious. I mean, if you see a couple of men going around smelling their motor car there's obviously a reason for it.

'We were just smelling it you know.'

'Naturally, but why? Is it on fire, are you burning?'

'Well, we thought—you know—a bit warm or something?'

'Let us try, open please.' He's a very good gendarme, we'll soon see what sort of a nose he's got for a bit of a whiff. We open the bonnet. Sniff, sniff. He's like a dog at a rabbit hole. Keen, alert, the bristle of his black moustache quivering under his questioning nostrils.

'Wonder if he's got any sort of clue, Tubby?'

'Don't think so.'

'It's all right I think,' I say to the gendarme.

'Naturally, but we must be careful.'

'Of course.' He sniffs his way around the car, he thought he picked up a trace of something around the rear off-side, but no.

'Everything is all right, I think,' he finally concludes.

'Naturally, but thank you very much.'

'Please don't mention it.'

'By the way, is there anywhere to stay near here?'

'Naturally, but there is a lot of traffic. A lot of noise.'

'Naturally. Does it go on all night?'

'Naturally, always a lot of traffic.'

'Oh, what a pity.'

'But if you want somewhere really quiet I know a very good place. It is first class.'

'Is it an hotel?'

'It is not really an hotel, no, but I think you will like it.' He looks at us closely and then at our beautiful motor car that he has personally sniffed all over and given a clean bill of smell. Yes, we would like where he's going to recommend. 'Yes, you leave on this road for two kilometres, there is a road by a bridge to the right. You go there for oh, one minute, there is the château.'

'The château?'

'Naturally.'

'We can stay there?'

'Naturally.'

And so we fetched up at the château. It wasn't the finest château that we had seen—you do get a bit blasé about châteaux in France, but as châteaux go this one went far enough to impose its personality upon you straight away. Rough, rugged, dour. No nonsense about this château. None of your frippery decoration around the lintels, no fine-turned urns or garden statues. No moat to mirror its stern profile, no shining swans to say that kings and queens were wont to sleep right there.

'Funny, doesn't seem to be a moat to this château.'

'No, it's overgrown I expect.'

Could be, for the vegetation struggles not far away, climbing up the trees, twisting itself in knots, trying to get its tendrils on the château. Obviously they have to go out and beat it back every few days. That convolvulus is dying to have a go at the south tower there. Yes, the old château is just about holding its own, I would say. Just about.

It's extraordinary sometimes how very neatly the character of a place builds itself even as you look at it. For as we looked at the château—not a soul about, not a sign of life, not a sign to say at which door we might be expected to knock—even as we looked a dog came trotting from somewhere behind the château.

You couldn't help noticing him because he was an English foxhound. It's the sort of dog you hardly ever see on its own. It's always along with a pack of yowlers. But this one was on his own and he wanted to be on his own, he had every reason to be on his own as quickly as possible, for although he was trying to pretend he wasn't hurrying at all he was really getting a bit of a move on because he was carrying in his mouth a fair-sized leg of lamb. And you knew at once that it wasn't his legitimate dinner. And he knew that we knew for as he trotted by he shot us a sidelong glance, like an old aristocrat that's fallen on dodgy times and just slipped someone a dud cheque. He almost said as he went by, 'Sure I can trust you gentlemen not to say anything about this.' And in a tick the vegetation closed around him and he was safe. Absolutely nothing could get at him in there. Never find him or the leg of lamb he'd nicked. And it's quite obvious that it wasn't the first prime cut that he'd swiped. He knew his way around the organisation of this place all right, an organisation that certainly had a very slack security system.

It was then that a door opened, a door at the top of a short flight of stone steps. A middle-aged dark lady stands there.

'Bonjour.'

'Bonjour, do you speak English?'

'A little.'

'We have been told that you may have some accommodation here, have you?'

'Please to come inside.' We pass into the château. It's been chopped up a bit during its long, dogged life. The first Duc did that, the second did that, the third ripped it all out, the fourth put some of it back. Then there was a bit of a fire and that bit was closed up for good . . . Nevertheless it's certainly a château at heart. The grand double doors are gracefully carved, the white marble floor with black diamond dots guide you to a gently sloping wooden staircase that groans and squeaks and turns twice upon itself before reaching the first landing. On the landing there's a little—well, it's a counter really. And madame moves neatly behind it.

She smiles, 'Ow long do you stay?'

'Well, just one night actually.'

'Oh, pity.' She had hoped for a little longer. 'Very well, if you would like to bring your baggage in I will send somebody to fetch it up here.'

'Thank you.'

'Thank you.'

We get our baggage and carry it into the marble hall. There waits for us, in a green apron, a porter. Quite the most extraordinary old porter that I've seen for many a long day. Well over six feet tall, he has the head of an old eagle, an old eagle that's had to give up flying and hunting because his eyes got misty and his feathers fell out. He looks down on us as he might on a couple of crouching rabbits. He doesn't think a lot of our baggage either. He's seen some real people come in through the château doors and *he* could tell us, the Duc du Quelquechose, the Marquis of Mal y Pense, the Comte de Pomme de Terre, Monsieur Chemin de Fer.

Oh yes, huh, we didn't come from the land of eagles, obviously we knew nothing of their castles, of the way they spread their wings and looked down on everything, the eagles, the Imperial eagles. You understand—looked down. The porter doesn't feel disposed to move our baggage. And because of this neither do we. We had reached what we call in English an impasse. They call it the same in France too, but it doesn't make any difference.

The old eagle turns his head towards the door to the left of the staircase. Madame's voice is trilling in the kitchen somewhere. *'Tenprederailment.'* And that does it. The old eagle's control is still around, he must obey it, he cocks his old head at our baggage again and rather grandly stoops, wraps a claw around the handle of the smallest briefcase and with a long loping sort of strut goes up the creaking stairs. With just one little briefcase! It's quite clear he's leaving the big baggage to us.

'Well, that was very nicely done, wasn't it?'

'Yes, you know, got a bad back I expect, not supposed to lift anything.'

'Yes. I've got an idea he's *never* had to lift anything.'

'Could be.'

We carry our baggage up behind the old eagle who now strides the gallery around the stairwell like a grand equerry preceding royal personages. Except that the royal personages have shed most of the dignity they ever had because they are walking lopsided, badly out of balance on account of the heavy baggage they are carrying. Looking back of course, we might perhaps have rumbled the situation a little sooner. An old château with the undergrowth advancing and retreating upon it every few weeks, the foxhound with a leg of lamb, the Madame and the old eagle porter. The Madame and the old eagle were the owners, probably with grand

177

titles, but the owners were suffering with more than a mild touch of Harry Shorters.

It's all the old eagle's fault we feel. Never able to run the place properly when there was a bit of money about. Full of ideas and wild schemes that he started but didn't pursue. Why, well people let you down, you know. And people don't give things time. You see if there had been more time and, er yes, a bit more money. Yes, a bit more money. But there wasn't. And what there was evaporated until Madame, we feel, asserted herself.

'It's no good, Henry, there's only one thing we can do—take in paying guests.'

'Oh good heavens no, how terribly suburban you are at times.'

'Well, what else can we do?'

'Well you know, that rabbit-fattening idea could really pay. If we sold only say—fifty rabbits a week to start with, that could make us quite a . . .'

'Henry, it's no good going on like that, you know what happened to the chickens and the pigs and the tomatoes.'

'Ah well, the tomatoes. Yes, but nobody could have foreseen *that*.'

'No, Henry, nobody could have foreseen that, so let us do something that we can foresee, paying guests.'

'What! Sleeping here?'

'Of course.'

'Oh, I can't stand the idea of people, strangers, coming in here and going to bed and all that. People we don't know, trippers, given the full run of the place, oh no, I can't stand the thought of that!'

But the thought is often worse than the reality. The old eagle has adapted fairly well, it's only at odd times that he objects to strangers, when they come in with their heavy baggage as a rule, for by the time we get to our grand apartment he has turned into a lofty, affable, mine host.

With a grand gesture he indicates our apartment like a conjurer affecting a grand illusion. He's accepted us as his guests, we're not all that bad, cheerful enough. He likes showing his guests their rooms, a bit like old times. Uhuhuh,

178

there's half a bottle of mineral water on a bedside shelf left by a previous guest! He slides over to it and with a casual laugh, *hahahaha*, slips it behind his back, we're not supposed to see that, or that—there's an old copy of the *Paris Soir* on the bed. He conjures that behind his back too. Hope there's nothing else left lying about, this will never do, oh no, there's an old hair curler on the dressing table! Oh dear, why don't they clear things away, why don't they, why don't they? But of course there aren't any 'they' nowadays, it's his job to keep the apartments dusted and tidy.

They used to do everything once upon a time: they did the silver, they did the garden, they did the polishing, they did the dusting. Now he is they, for they have gone and he has to be all of they now.

He looks at the hair curler and laughs, *hahahah*. He has to put the old mineral water bottle down to pick the hair curler up. *Hahaha*.

I couldn't have known at that point how I added to the poignant irony of the situation when I said, 'Oh yes, mineral water yes, could you let us have a bottle of mineral water some time please?'

Well, I still thought he was the porter and not the acting aristocratic porter.

He put the hair curler in his green apron pocket, picked up the bottle and said, '*Hahahaha*, you can get it yourself at the bar, *hahahaha*.' And he chuckled off around the gallery. 'Catch me taking them mineral water, *hahahaha*!'

That's all he could do, laugh. It was the best thing to do in the world of grand muddle in which he had always lived. He wasn't exactly laughing later that evening though, when we walked around the château before dinner and heard the old eagle and Madame having a bit of a ding-dong in the kitchen. But a very genteel ding-dong.

'But Henry, are you sure?'

'Yes, I'm sure. Of course I'm sure, I put it there—on the table.'

'Well, it's not here now.'

'No, I can see that.'

'Well, a leg of lamb can't walk.'

'No, a leg of lamb can't walk, *hahaha*, funny that—leg of lamb can't walk—*hahaha*. I don't know, I brought everything from the car and put it on the table, onions, beans and the leg of lamb.'

But the leg of lamb, of course, lay deep in the château jungle mutilated and muddy, and beside it lay a foxhound who'd long since learned to fend for himself in a world of dignified muddle.

But of course muddle has its charms. And if you begin to think about muddle then sometimes the most muddled things in appearance are the clearest cut and unmuddled. Well, think of the muddle made by that incredible French postman. His name was Cheval. Le facteur Cheval. The postman Cheval. Now he had a large garden at the back of his house and he didn't do a lot about it until he had a dream, a dream that set everything in his mind in motion and in order. For his dream told him that he must build a palace. An ideal palace. That's all. Go and do it. And in 1879 the postman Cheval started to build his palace in his garden. Now with his dream must also have come a vision of some sort, for his palace is like nothing hitherto known on this earth. He must have recalled all the scenes from the *Arabian Nights* that he read as a child, every bit of illustration from every magazine he'd ever chanced upon, Babylonian palaces, Swiss chalets, Roman viaducts, Turkish mosques, Indian temples, Chinese pagodas and Victorian villas and he bunged them all together. He bunged it with goats and elephants and birds and long-legged people twenty feet high, he bunged them in with strange vacant faces that are every bit as bewildering as the people who stare at them. And he built it all with little bits of stone and cement. He collected the stones from all around and brought them home in a wheelbarrow and used them as part of his monumental doodle. Bit by bit he built this colossal coral reef, well it's thirty yards long and fifteen yards wide. It was his dream. And he saw it very clearly in stone and cement. He built it out of his own head, his own thoughts materialised in stone and cement.

There seems to be no rhyme or reason for what goes on. He just had to do it. It took him thirty-three years to build and he built it on his own. And when he'd finished, that was that, there were no afterthoughts, no additions, nothing, that was it. Done. He knew. He inscribed it.

The work of one man: thirty-three years, ten thousand days, ninety-two thousand hours.

He also delivered letters. The facteur Cheval who felt that he had to account for every second of his life in stone and cement.

And what looks like the most appalling nonsense of muddle to us must have been as clear as sunshine to him. But that's the strange thing about muddle. There's muddle and there's muddle.

CHAPTER FIFTEEN

From Beer Garden to Wine Festival

One of the greatest blessings in this life is one of the most natural of all things—sleep. Sweet, beautiful sleep. It's wonderful, isn't it? That is if you can sleep. So let me tell you about myself. I find that there's nothing like a nice chat about me, don't you? Well, I can sleep. I can do a heavy deep-down sleep for seven or eight hours, or a light little shut-eye for ten or fifteen minutes, or I can do a quick, sitting-bolt-upright, two-minute nap. Not only that, I can perform any of these natural acts in a feather bed, on top of a bus or on a hard oak church pew. As if that isn't enough to torment those who suffer from insomnia I have to add that I can also do any of the aforementioned things in most parts of the world. North and South America, Scandinavia, Japan, the Islands of the South Pacific and India . . .

Ah India, now *there's* a place for sleep. Wherever you go you will find people unashamedly asleep. For in India when you've finished your work or you can't think of anything to do you just tilt right over where you happen to be and go to sleep, under a tree, in a field or at the bus stop.

Sleep is a beautiful condition that costs the National Health Service of this country millions of pounds to achieve. For living highly unnatural lives as we do, we have to take pills to make us sleep. Well, lots of us do. So, still going on about me for another tick or two—if you don't mind—I'm very lucky, for I can sleep. Perhaps I have a subconscious desire to be shot of this wicked world, I don't know. But I have no need of sleeping pills. Old Morpheus and me are the best of pals. I've only to glance in his direction and he clouts

me with his velvet hammer and I'm out. Sleeping pills, I've
no need for them.

I've never had one—oh yes I have, they made me take one
once in hospital.

The nurse said, 'Now I'll just get you a sleeping pill and
you can settle down for the night.'

And I said, 'I don't want one.'

And she said, 'Oh yes you do, I'm going to get one.'

And she went away to get a sleeping pill. When she came
back I was asleep and she had to wake me up to give me the
sleeping pill—which was pretty daft, you must agree.

So you see, when I come to the end of the day I come to the
end of the day. Yes, but not here. For in Germany the day
has no end. Dear old Morpheus had no passport to
Germany. I don't think anybody ever goes to sleep in
Germany. Well, they might nod off for five minutes around
about tea time but they're up and about all night. And
they're up and about with such noisy things: tramcars,
railway trains, cracked cathedral bells, clocks, scooters,
police cars and ambulances.

And then of course there are the roisterers. The Germans
do terribly love a good roister. And a good roister is all right
if you happen to be right there in the middle of it helping with
the roist, but if you happen to be lying stiff and tense in bed
with your hair on end and your eyes wide open like a
frightened cat you would dearly love a potful of something to
damp down the roisterers or a sleeping pill for yourself. But I
doubt if it would do much good, only the stone deaf could
sleep here.

Of course the trouble is that the only hotels are right in the
middle of the towns. And the only bedrooms, it seems, are
located about four feet away from the tram track and the
tram stop. The trams come moaning in and out all
night—*mmmmmmmganggangmmmmmmm. Squeeeeee*. All motor
cars come around corners like that in Germany: *squeeeee*.
Must be a car of crooks on the run, *squeeeee*, there're the cops
after them, *heehawheehawheehaw*, there goes the ambulance
braying like a donkey, *gongongongongong*, the cathedral clock
slapping his old clapper for three o'clock.

Barkbarkbark — squeeee — mmmmmmgang-
mmmmmmgang — inviederholdergerverlumd insteinve-
lumst — mmmmmmmganggang — squeeeeee — insteinverlumst insteinverlumst — hahaha — mmmmm-
gangmmmmm — heehawheehawheehaw . . .

And one town is much the same as another. For about a
week now Tubby Foster and I have been booking in at hotels
with accommodation overlooking the tramtracks.

'It's a pity really, Tubby, I don't want to grow to dislike
tramcars because I do dearly love the tramcar.'

'Yes I know, so do I. You know, it might be a good idea if
we booked an all-night ticket on the tram.'

'You think we might go to sleep?'

Well it's worth a try, mmm, but some towns are better
than others. Heidelberg wasn't too bad as far as I remember.
There were noises in the night there that were actually very
pleasant. Steam trains. Yes, steam trains puffing the rails,
puffpuffpuff. Dear old steam trains, nearly forgotten all
about them.

It was rather a nice hotel at Heidelberg. Very helpful
young waiter there, helped us to translate the menu, for the
German language—for me at any rate—is a difficult one. I
can't really take it seriously. It is difficult to believe that
people invented such extraordinary noises as a means of
communication. Of course, if I stayed here long enough no
doubt I might come to grips with it, for languages and
dialects are infectious after a time. So I will really try to
concentrate on this menu with this young waiter.

'Now, what is this here? How do you say it: Kartofell and
Gemuse? You can't eat a Kartoffel and a Gemüse can you,
and this, Schnitzel, that's veal—right?'

'Yes, that's right. This is a sort of veal and it is fried with
breadcrumbs and we are also serving it with potatoes and
vegetables.'

'Oh well that sounds nice. You speak very good English.'

'I ought to be able to speak it quite well, because I am
coming from Guildford.'

'From Guildford, what, you stayed there?'

'No no, I was born there, went to school there.'

'Oh, I see, but your parents were German?'

'No no, I am absolutely English, but what is happening now is that I am here for two years to learn the hotel business. I am particularly interested in restaurant management and I will probably do a stint in the kitchens although it's quite difficult to say because I don't know if my father wants me to stay over here all that long time.' And as he talks his German accent fades away. 'It's a bit of a bind actually because the old man's got quite a big hotel you know and, well there's a hell of a lot to do and he's got labour problems you know, can't get the staff and that, well you know, he keeps writing to me to say he could do with me back home but I don't really want to go. I like this place, suits me fine.'

It's quite extraordinary the way he's been infected by the German accent and loses it as he talks to us. No doubt the language of the kitchen is English here. A sort of middle-European English—that is vy everybody is tokking like zis and making vis the knives and spoons and vis the forks and chopping up the cabbige.

It's very understandable when you come to think of it. I remember I once spent a few weeks in Southern Ireland and that after a while I found myself chatting away in the hotel bar as nice as you like. Would you believe that now? I suppose it is much cosier to imitate the sounds around you rather than make a noise that is out of place. And the young waiter in the Heidelberg hotel quickly transposes himself from his German context to his South of England one. He hasn't been to England for two years, doesn't know or care very much about what is happening there, and then he says, 'Fine, I'll bung this order through right away because we've got a coach party coming in for dinner in a minute and all hell will be let loose, you see.'

And all hell is let loose. The block-booked block busters come surging into the dining room and the air is thick with Kartoffel and Gemüse and Schnitzel and Sauerkraut and Wurst. Our waiter races about with dishes of stodge and spoonfuls of splodge. He is entirely absorbed with his work and has no time to chat. He has retreated behind that solid, impersonal barrier that protects those who serve the public.

Everybody will be served equally, no personal favours granted anywhere. We are too flippin' busy to bother with you, missus.

And he brings us our coffee with a serious and distant look on his face. As he tinkles the coffee spoons in the saucers I can't help marvelling at what he said ten minutes ago. He said: 'We've got a coach party coming in for dinner in a minute and all hell will be let loose, you see. All hell will be let loose, you see.' For as he now stands with the two silver pots in his hands he says: 'Are you wanting your coffee black or vis milk?'

'Black, please.'

'Sank you; and you sir, are you wanting black or vis milk?'

'Black please.'

'Sank you, sir.' The South of England is a thousand miles away as he pours the coffee in Heidelberg.

There's a very striking castle at Heidelberg and funnily enough it has been struck three times by lightning. It stands high above the town overlooking the River Neckar, a tributary of the Rhine. It is a situation of great beauty. For the River Neckar flows through a woody ravine under the mediaeval bridges of Heidelberg and then eases out into the great flat valley that the Rhine has ironed out for itself. A valley of silt and industry. A valley that grows tobacco and asparagus and grapes and potatoes and vegetables, the old Kartoffel and Gemüse. A valley that blows and blooms and belches bilious breath, for in the distance the factory chimneys of Mannheim pump up their daily offering of smoke and choke. It's a most extraordinary valley. We drive along the flat roads through acres of asparagus all run to seed, splattered red with berries, past fields of tobacco and potato. They are picking the spuds and gathering the deadly weed and the farm carts rumble the roads rich and heavy. There's a load of tobacco ahead turning into the drying sheds alongside the road.

'Tubby, don't you think that cart should have written on the side of it a government warning that cigarette smoking is a danger to your health?'

'Why not? I think that motor cars should have government warnings pasted on them too. "This car is a danger to life." '

'Yes, and on flick knives. "This knife can kill you if you're not careful." '

'Exactly.'

'And on bottles of whisky.'

'Yes, I wonder why they don't warn us about whisky? We ought to be warned about whisky you know, killed many a good bloke, whisky, especially if he smoked as well.'

'Mmm, 'course if they wanted to stop people smoking they could easily.'

'How?'

'Stop growing tobacco.'

'I suppose so. It's strange how we tinker with life's problems and refuse to deal with them.'

'Yes, still, it's the money.'

Yes, the money. If we stopped growing tobacco what about the revenue? What indeed, we've tinkered up a situation that would make a cat laugh. We allow a nation to become addicted to the smoking of tobacco, slap a thumping great tax on it, shovel up the money with a chuckle and tell everybody that they are really being very silly going on like this. And the tobacco wagons trundle over the fine Rhine silt, gathering up the innocent leaves. And every leaf a cough and a hoick and a dab in the hand for the Chancellor . . . Cough. Thank you very much but don't do it. Cough. Thank you very much, you really shouldn't you know. Cough . . .

Sorry to keep on like this, but the River Rhine winds its way through a great concentration of life's problems. And life's biggest problem is of course money. Making stuff into things to sell for money to buy more stuff to make into things. Everything else is secondary. Money is first, foremost and final. Life is the balance of payments and a healthy economy that makes everything else unhealthy. For hereabouts the water of the Rhine has become a cold chemical consommé.

You do get a shock or two as you travel around. You have no doubt heard of Liebfraumilch? Liebfraumilch, a white wine that is respected and swilled by many. Its very name is the epitome of goodness, and indeed the vineyard where grow the grapes for the Liebfraumilch was once no doubt a very pleasant spot. A vineyard spread about around a church just on the outskirts of the city of Worms, years ago a holy and venerated spot. And it still is but only just, for the city of Worms has spread and all but engulfed the vineyard. The vineyard has had to put up a high wire fence around itself for protection. The railway has cut a way through it. A great trunk road has hacked a dual carriageway across it. And the mysterious tanks and gasometers of industry stand on its fringes. But it's hanging out. There's enough industrial menace here to make the grapes wither and the dear old milch curdle. But the vineyard is hanging out. It's surrounded but it will never be taken. For if there's one man who can stand up to a bad industrialist it's a good boozer. For once it seems there's a shift in the balance of priorities.

So when next you sip a glass of cool Liebfraumilch astonish your friends by not applying the usual adjectives like fruity, elegant or discreet and just say, very brave wine this, probably the bravest and most stubborn wine on the Rhine. And there's a lot of wine on the Rhine. Vineyards all along the road, green grapes growing on the gentle rolling slopes where the river takes it easy. It's no trouble for it to glide through the soft silt here, but by the time it gets to Rüdesheim it has to pull itself together to force its way through a formidable barrier.

When you get a powerful river and a stubborn lot of rock in conflict you get scenery. For this is the bit of the Rhine that people come to see. It's the bit where the battered castles stand dominating the river from the rocky heights, it's the bit where the Rhine slithers through the towering rocks at a dangerous frightening rip, it's the bit that swills past the rock where once sat a maiden calling to the boatmen and luring them to their death on the wicked rocks, she sat going: 'Ooo ooo ooo ooo, Charlie, Charlie, can you spare a minute Charlie, ooo ooo.'

It's the bit that the bad Barons battled over. It's the bit that made Richard Wagner go pompompompom. It's the bit that you've got to travel by boat and be humbled by the sheer force of the river and rock, it's the bit that you've got to get on top of, right on top of the cliffs, and wonder at the beautiful gorge the river has carved for itself. Oh, it's quite a bit of river.

Grapes grow all up the staircase sides of the ravine. Pleasure paddle-steamers dabble up and down all day. Yes, steamers with sweet smooth pistons, steel conrods and bright brass big ends, and black funnels lisping wisps of steam. And on the narrow ledge of the river bank the railway trains scamper all day long, on both sides of the Rhine. And they are never still for a minute.

That's why we thought twice about staying at Rüdesheim. For apart from all the usual German night noises there are the railways, not just passenger trains, oh no, but goods trains half a mile long tramping about all night. For a good deal of Germany's industry travels up and down the Rhine, not only in the barges but on the railway trains. And the railway trains rattle right along the front at Rüdesheim. I call it the front at Rüdesheim because it is rather like a seaside promenade and it certainly attracts the visitors.

For this is the place to come if you want to see a good chunk of scenery and whoop it up a bit. It's the ideal place for the quick weekend if you like that sort of thing. And there are many that do. Well, to start with there's a rather attractive funicular that carried you away out of the town and across the vineyards. It passes an hour or two. A trip down the river passes an hour or two. A conducted tour around the brandy distillery passes an hour or two . . .

So what do you do with the rest of your quick weekend? Ah well, you can get yourself into a fine old state if you don't watch it. For in Rüdesheim there is a most peculiar lane or alley called the Drosselgasse, Thrush Lane or Thrush Alley, the Drosselgasse. It is a narrow alleyway of pubs, beer gardens, drinking dens and night clubs. The street of a thousand thick heads. For you can drink here any time of the day or night, and if you're chucked out of one boozer you fall into another one. And every boozer blares out the oh-be-joyful music. Real live music with real live musicians, combinations of two, three, four, five or more instrumentalists: *omphahoomhahoompahgeydarey*. In the Drosselgasse there are at least thirty-five little orchestras blowing out the jollity, *tarararara oomphaoompah*, and the street is crammed with those who have come to enjoy themselves.

And a lot of them do. You can see them rollocking away in the beer gardens, roistering it up in the drinking dens, *insteinverlumst hahaha oooooo*. Pub after pub after pub, *insteinverlumst hahaha*. It's quite fascinating, it's like walking through one of Hogarth's nightmares. Gin Alley. And on either side and in every bar the rakes are progressing very nicely, thank you.

It is a most dangerous alley. Not that you'd get mugged or knifed, oh no—it's absolutely safe as far as that is concerned—it's dangerous because it is charged with temptation. Yes, temptation. I know that sounds old fashioned and a bit prudish, and there's very little that will tempt me nowadays. I think I've sampled most of the so-called delights of this life. But to the innocent and unaware this must be condensed temptation. The mythical characters of the tempters are everywhere, slopping their beer mugs at you, waving you to come on in. They are having a dickens of a time, come on in, don't stand out there in the alley looking so blinking miserable and pious, come on in and wallow and laugh and sing and forget, *insteinverlumst hahaha ooo*.

If you can walk from one end of the Drosselgasse to the other without having a drink, then you are avoiding the temptation all right and you can't help feeling a bit smug. Perhaps that's why so many people wander up and down the Drosselgasse night and day. It's always jammed with people just meandering in a lost sort of way to the top of the alley and then back down again. Many of them are not aware of the temptation that lurks so close but they know it's something a bit peculiar.

Tubby Foster and I wander up one evening and stop outside one of the beer gardens. We have to stop because there's a small group of English tourists blocking the way. They are having a quiet English discussion.

'Well what do you think, should we go in?'

'Well it looks a bit expensive, doesn't it?'

'It's about the same as all the others.'

'What do you think we can have to drink?'

'Well, I think you can have pretty well anything, you know.'

'I don't want wine.'

'No, well you needn't.'

'If you have wine you have to have the whole bottle, I think.'

'Yes, well there're six of us, aren't there?'

'Those fellows over by the band look as though they've had plenty.'

'Well, shall we try somewhere else?'

And they go to try somewhere else. But an hour later they are still wandering and wondering because Tubby Foster and I sit in that wicked beer garden with a pot of beer each and watch the ramblers in the alley. This is the third time the English group have gone by. They peer at us all with great suspicion, especially at the fellows over by the band. They've had more than plenty. No, they're not coming in. Yes? No? Well, two of the party appear to want to come in but the other four don't. The two who want to come in are a bit put out by this and get slightly sulky with the other four. And half an hour and two turns of the Drosselgasse later the whole party is sulking. And the fellows by the band are carrying out one of their number who seems to have lost his balance.

But if the Drosselgasse is a dangerous place in which to dawdle, it is but a kindergarten compared to a vine fest. A vine fest or a wine festival sets out to be a pleasant festivity in praise and honour of the grape. And wine festivals are held in the autumn in many of the little towns along the grape-growing parts of the Rhine.

Now the grape is a very funny fruit, very funny fruit indeed. A beautiful symbol of abundance, I grant you, but a tricky little devil. Well the growing of him is tricky, he needs the right amount of sun, the right amount of rain, he has to be sprayed to keep him free of the fungus, he's picked and trodden and bottled and watched and turned and tasted and tested to produce a drink so subtle, so refreshing, so satisfying. A drink that so pleasantly draws you back a few paces from the cliff-edge of harsh reality.

A wonderful fruit really, is the grape, if he's treated properly. For the grape must above all things be appreciated. It's got to be appreciated. The moment you cease to appreciate the grape and treat him like any old glass of tipple he will let loose a vengeance on one and all that has to be seen to be believed. And if you don't believe me, visit a wine festival on the Rhine one wet September day and get a load of the havoc the wine will work on those who lose their appreciation. To start with a wine festival is a very pretty affair. They decorate the village with dark green foliage and flowers and flags. They put up marquees and trestle tables with table cloths. They hang streamers from pillar to post. They drag out the sausages and Sauerkraut. They put on the Sunday best and summon the German band and trundle out the barrels and the bottles.

It's all good clean fun to start with, I imagine, but we didn't get there at the start. We got there at about half past three in the afternoon just as it was beginning to drizzle. We parked the car outside the village and walked up towards the village square. And then this life-size rag doll came hurtling down the road towards us. Except that it wasn't a rag doll—it was a very floppy man. When he passed us every bit of control had left him. He was just like a rag doll. He had started off on his way and developed a nasty stagger in all directions, and now, desperately trying to correct this terrible stagger, he was gaining momentum and practically cartwheeling downhill. Legs and arms flying. A rag doll being shaken by a terrier.

He came to a thundering stop when he hit a brick wall trying to avoid a group of men coming up the hill. They picked him up and dusted him down and, hanging on to them, he came back up the hill to join the wine festival once again. He was still good for a couple more bottles, he thought. But I don't think he made it for we saw him half an hour later out for the count near the bandstand. It's quite astonishing the effect that wine has on body control. I've never seen it demonstrated as actively as at this wine festival.

People falling about all over the place.

Not everybody of course, for it's rather like the Drossel-gasse, there are those that over-indulge and those that don't. And those that don't over-indulge stand about and chat in the rain underneath umbrellas. The sound of wine glasses crashing and trestle tables collapsing moves them not. That young man has collapsed on to a trestle table. The road swills with wine and broken glass. And do you know, we talked to him just half an hour ago. He spoke a little English, wanted a little practice . . . He was all right then, but the wine poleaxed him—wallop—like that. They lay him to rest on the town hall steps.

And the rain drips and drips and the railway trains pound up and down the railway lines beside the Rhine, *blblblblbl*. Still I will say this for a good vine fest: if you are troubled by noises in the night and you can't sleep and you have no sleeping pills, put in a short burst at the vine fest just before bedtime. But only a short burst.

CHAPTER SIXTEEN

The Wildlife of Mexico

Wherever we go the zopelottis go too. There was a time when we used to stare at the zopelottis and shudder a bit. But not now, we've got used to the zopelottis. Well, that is as used as you can ever get to a zopelotti. But as long as Mexico is Mexico the zopelottis will be there because the zopelotti is a protected bird. You are not allowed to shoot a zopelotti or harm a zopelotti or interfere with the zopelotti in any way at all, for the zopelotti is a vulture and vultures in Mexico are very necessary. They are the unpaid freelance refuse collectors, the diligent dustmen, the casual carrion disposal squad, the ever-vigilant death-watch undertaker. The zopelotti. Oh yes, very useful bird is the old zopelotti.

I don't mind telling you that if it weren't for the zopelottis the rates in Mexico would be up by about 8 pence in the pound. Well, they're on the go the whole time. They don't miss a thing. The slightest sign of a tragedy and they are there.

They were there in a twink when that dog was nearly done to death. We were driving along a pretty fast highway, skiddling along past the prickly pears. A motor car was in front of us—about a hundred yards in front—when suddenly a long lurching dog, a sort of cross between a greyhound and a hyena, comes slowly ambling up a low embankment and walks absentmindedly in front of the car ahead of us. Oh dear, there goes another innocent. Because there is a pretty constant massacre of the innocents. There are so many of them. They are all on their own. They have no one to tell them, guide them or train them or feed them. So only the very cunning, super-crafty survive, the rest die or get killed. Quite frequently you see dead dogs by the wayside with the black-coated zopelottis in attendance and now here goes another one.

The car in front goes into a skid. Hot blue smoke screams from his back wheels, the car slithers sideways and crashes into a bridge that crosses the road, just missing the dog. Oh these innocents—they're not really to blame, but here's one wrecked car and what about the man inside? No, he's all right. We pull up behind. He climbs out of his smashed-up car.

'You all right, señor?'

'Si, si, si, Santa Maria!'

We examine his car. It's badly bent in places but it looks as though it will still go. We pull it back on to the road. The lucky dog watches us with a mystified expression on his face: these human beings, I don't know, go flying around in tin cans, banging into bridges—must be barmy. Don't know what they see in it. They'll kill themselves if they're not careful . . .

And he lopes off back the way he has come just as the first zopelotti rattles down on to a tree at the side of the road and folds his black undertakers' wings ready for the post mortem. There's something so horribly business-like in the way they fold their wings one after the other. They are so sure they will be needed, so confident of their own expert surgical ability. Like surgeons they know exactly how a body is put together and, therefore, they know exactly how to take it apart. And before they commence an operation they always seem to ask for the case history of the patient first of all. Ah yes: dog, mongrel, aged four, emaciated, some signs of mange here and there, vagrant—oh yes, obviously a vagrant, no signs of identification. Cause of death? Oh, accidental, caused by a heavy vehicle of some sort no doubt, probably inflicting severe damage to the liver and kidney, still we'll soon find out, better call in another opinion or two—not that I couldn't manage on my own. Still . . . And a couple more zopelottis rattle down into the tree.

As vultures go they are not bad looking birds. Fairly small

and neat and they don't appear to suffer from indigestion as much as their African colleagues. Still, no pickings here today, zopelottis, better luck next time. But they're always around wherever we go.

They weren't very far away the day Tubby Foster disappeared. One second he was there and the next there he was gone. Well, we were looking for a shop that sold cigarettes and these sort of shops are not always easy to identify right away. They sell cigarettes in a variety of different shops—you can never be suré which—and we're wandering up this hot street. A hot white street absolutely saturated with heat, gawping about looking for a cigarette sign.

'You know, I don't think they need to sell cigarettes here. They probably grow their own tobacco, roll their own cigarettes and so they—where's he gone! Where is he?'

'Hey!' Tubby's voice appears to come from right beside me. 'Hey!'

'Where are you?'

'Hey!'

'Good heavens, what are you doing down there?'

There's not very much of Tubby showing actually, just the top half of him sticking up out of the road. The rest of him has gone down a drain. It's a weird sight, the top half of a torso sticking up out of the road. No wonder a couple of zopelottis clattered down on to a nearby roof almost immediately. They thought this was very interesting.

'What the heck has happened?'

'I don't know. I was walking along beside you and there was no cover on this drain and I went down—give us a hand.'

It is, of course, the perfect comic joke. Every week in my old comic paper Tiger Tim or Marzipan the Magician would take the cover off a manhole and catch somebody. Someone who needed to be taught a lesson, someone who wanted paying out. Take the cover off, here he comes—*hahahaha*, got him! Very good that.

Naturally I never really believed that it could happen. But it has happened here. I can't believe it. Luckily for Tubby

he's fallen into a 36-inch drain and he's got a 40-inch
waistline and that's why he's stuck.

'Come on, give us a hand.'

'Who took the cover off? Marzipan the Magician?'

'Don't muck about, come on, I can't get out!'

It's not easy rescuing people who have got stuck in
manholes or coal holes or drains. The people in *Tiger Tim's
Weekly* always went right down to the coal cellar but Tubby is
stuck pretty tight halfway and I can't move him. Two
cheerful Mexican gentlemen come along while I'm heaving
away. Do I need assistance? If they would be so kind. What
has happened? My Spanish is very limited and I haven't got
my phrase book with me. Pity, because this is a really
phrase-book situation. It's sure to be in the book with all the
other tom fool phrases: 'My friend has become stuck in the
drain—pray help me dislodge him.'

After all, there are lots of daft phrases in the book. There's
one that goes: 'Are you going to stuff it with cement?' Are you
going to stuff it with cement? Now when would you want to
say a thing like that? Ah, but you never know. In the light of
what's happened it's quite reasonable to suppose that I
would find in the phrasebook, 'My friend has become stuck
in the drain—pray help me dislodge him.' Sure to be in the
book. Still, I haven't got it.

I do a small piece of mime and the three of us manage to
draw Tubby out of the drain, like a cork out of a bottle. *Phew*,
quite a vintage drain too.

'Gracias, gracias.'

'Please don't mention it; any time you are in similar
difficulties only too pleased.'

'Gracias, gracias.'

'*Phew*, that was a near go, Johnny.'

'Yes, the old zopelottis were queuing up for you, you
know.'

'I know, I saw them. They are everywhere.'

They were not so much in evidence though when we took
the road to Veracruz. It was a fine morning—when we saw
him smiling by the roadside. We wanted to help him but we
couldn't. There he stood at the side of the road with a great

galvanised bucket full of raw red meat. He wanted a lift, he said, only a couple of kilometres, but the bucket was heavy and the sun was hot and the flies were buzzing black and disgusting. It wasn't much to ask, was it, a lift for a couple of kilometres? I could see his point all right, after all, we had a motor car. Be reasonable, he hadn't. We had only to squeeze up a little bit and he could squash in with his big bucket of meat and in ten minutes he would be at his village and we could go on our way. Oh yes, of course the flies would have to come too, I mean—where there's meat there's flies. What can you expect, be reasonable.

He had just that sort of expression on his face, helped along by one of those devastating Mexican smiles, be reasonable.

'We ought to help him, really.'

'Yes, but *phew*, I don't think I could stomach that. Can't you put our point of view to him?'

Well, we know what our point of view is but he would never understand. Our point of view is simple. The temperature at the moment is getting on for 100 degrees, the car is like a tin oven, you could fry an egg on the roof if you felt that it would achieve anything. There's just enough room for the two of us and we are streaming with perspiration. Not only that, Tubby and I are both suffering from the after-effects of Montezuma's Revenge and we are being rather foolhardy blundering about in the middle of Mexico with querulous stomachs as it is. And now this bucket of raw meat and the black haze of flies. He's a nice enough man but he's in a bit of a pickle himself. Well, he's a hardworking bloke, he's already mucked out the pigs this morning (you don't have to be a bloodhound to wind that) and he's milked the cow, and he was going to put on a decent pair of trousers this morning and have a bit of a wash and a shave, but you know what it is what with one thing and another you don't seem to get time and before you know where you are another hot month has slipped by . . .

Come on, be reasonable. There's that attractive face smiling in the shade of a great curly grimy sombrero. Be reasonable. So you see it was a tremendous relief to us when a dirty old rattle-bang lorry juddered along, going the way that the bucket of meat wanted to go. The bucket of meat didn't lose a second. He wasn't going to muck about with these namby-pambies any more. He shouts out 'Ola'. The lorry squeaks and stops and the bucket of meat goes galloping after it. Adios, adios.

'Well, I'm glad he's got a lift.'

'Yes, so am I.'

'I wish he'd taken all his flies with him.'

'Yes, he's left a couple of hundred clawing about on the windscreen.'

'Come on, let's get going and blow them out.'

'Hey, what's going on? The lorry hasn't moved yet.'

'Why?'

The bucket of meat has clambered aboard and settled himself down beside his buzzing bucket, but what are they waiting for? Look, they're waiting for that little old lady there. Oh yes. A little old lady in a white sombrero comes belting down the road carrying a bucket. And it's a bucket of meat. No doubt about it. Just look at the flies streaming behind it like smoke from a dirty chimney stack.

'Odd isn't it?'

'Yes, very odd—here comes another.' Another tough-looking countryman with a smoky-chimney bucket races for the lorry. And now a little boy stumbles with a bucket. He's having a difficult time. Well, the bucket is so heavy he has to keep changing hands and the bucket bangs his little legs and it upsets the flies who get irritable and smoulder around him as he staggers to the lorry. But he makes it and they all scramble aboard and away they go.

'Well, what do you make of that, Watson?'

'Elementary, they've been getting meat from somewhere in buckets!'

'Yes, but where?' I mean, we are right in the middle of the country, we are well on our way to the port of Veracruz. We are nearly down to sea level—that's why it's so hot. We've been on the go since fairly early this morning driving through the heat and the butterflies.

You see—we are so used to the butterflies we never even

mention them now. Well, if you've seen one butterfly we have seen 5,000 million. It really is a most fantastic sight. It is a plague of butterflies. They are butterflies about the size of our cabbage white only they are bright orange and bright yellow. And it's all rather upsetting because you simply cannot avoid slaughtering goodness knows how many of these butterflies. How can you drive a motor car through 5,000 million flittering butterflies without doing some to death? They have no thought of motor cars as they tremble in the roadway, quivering with the excitement of the mad-nuptual morning and as the sun climbs higher in the sky the sticky black tarmac road slowly turns into a winding mosaic pave of orange and yellow tragedy. Such a pretty tragedy, all those dead mariposas. Such a pretty word for a butterfly, mariposa. But for every mariposa set still in the delicate coloured mosaic there are thousands flipping about. It's like driving through a constant shower of yellow and orange confetti, the wedding of the mariposas.

And it was while we were wiping some dead mariposas from our windscreen that the bucket of meat came along and asked for a lift.

'Well, you haven't solved the mystery of the buckets of meat.'

'No. They all came from over there.'

Over there, well back from the road is a big tree. A large, dark green cypress of some sort that spreads its branches and commands full use of all the ground it can keep in the shade. 'Well, let's go and have a look.'

We walk over to the tree. It's buzzing with flies. It's quite extraordinary. The tree is a butcher's shop. Yes, there standing in the shade of this great tree is a butcher and he's got all his meat hung in the tree: a couple of sides of stringy beef hanging on ropes; an old sheep that's been hacked into gobbets and strung about where the branches sweep low and handy; a long and rangy goat swings quietly in eight separate lumps, all the lumps swinging strangely in rhythm together as though the old billy was subconsciously still plodding the well-worn goat tracks. Dotted here and there are a few chops tied to twigs, a dull blob of liver, a heart or two, some pale pink sloppy hanging lights, and laced casually in the branches setting the whole thing off nicely are yards and yards of trailing chitterlings. It is a sort of ghoulish Christmas tree. A sick joke Christmas tree.

'Oh come on Tubby, be reasonable, it's a butcher's shop.'

'Yes, but all these animals hanging in the tree look as though they've been lynched.'

'Be reasonable, meat is meat. The trouble is you're so spoiled, getting your meat all sealed up in plastic bags with a ticket on it and all the guff and rubbish about hygiene and humane behaviour—come off it. Be reasonable.'

'I am reasonable, I am reasonable, it's a nice butcher's shop in a tree right in the country with a jolly butcher sharpening his knife as all butchers do.'

Except that he hasn't a roof over his head or a fridge to his name, just a chopping block and a table and a bucket of water. It's no good—how can you see it as a butcher's shop? He's spilled some water on the dry ground just by his chopping block and hundreds of mariposas are flittering and settling at the edge of the tiny pool to drink. Every time the butcher makes a movement near them they go flickering up amongst the hanging carcasses, hundreds of pretty paper snippets of orange and yellow confetti. We just stand and watch, fascinated by this incredible picture of the dark green tree and the jolly butcher and his flashing knives, the red meat, the dull blood and the butterflies, the mariposas. There are one or two customers squatting with their buckets waiting to be served and the butcher keeps up a nice line of jolly country butcher chat. Can't hear what he's saying—I suppose he speaks the equivalent of a Wiltshire Spanish.

'Ah buenos dias Señora Sanchez, que quiere, poco de carne? Si, si, poco de carne, circa de dos kilos? Si, dos kilos, momentito momentito, y Señor Sanchez como esta Señor Sanchez? Bueno bueno, si si y los ninos, buenos buenos mucha gracias Señora Sanchez, dos kilos mas y menos dos kilos es momentito momentito, dos kilos es nueve pesos, mucho gracias hahaha, mucho gracias.'

He flops the meat into her bucket. Well, what do you want

to muck about with wrapping paper for, only litter up the countryside like those over-civilised people up in the north.

'Right, next please, Señora Mendoza what can we do for you today?'

'I don't know, it's a job to know what to get.' Señora Mendoza gazes up into the gallows tree, the butcher gazes with her. 'What do you recommend today?'

'What do we recommend today? Why bless you, we can recommend everything, bit of shin that'll stew up lovely?'

'All right then, a bit of shin.'

The butcher ambles over to his chopping block, the mariposas fluttering up and settling as he passes, and we wander back to our big tin oven and roast all the way to Veracruz.

There is a bit of a breeze moving about at Veracruz but even so the heat is a moist heat and it's not what you'd call comfortable. The most comfortable things in Veracruz, I imagine, are the frigate birds that float about high in the sky and the tearaway urchins that dive all day long into the harbour. Everybody seems to have all the time in the world at Veracruz and you need all the time in the world because the slightest physical movement and you start to drip like a sour lemon under pressure. The best thing to do is to sit still and sip at something long and cool in one of the pavement cafés in the square. Everybody sits and sips and talks and the marimba bands wander from café to café. These marimba bands are quite extraordinary. Well, there are so many of them and they're about all day long wearing their great curly sombreros.

But it's at night when the big square at Veracruz really sizzles with all the gay carnival characters, all the up and coming, all the down and out, all the drinkers, all the scroungers, the beggars, the sellers, the little chiclets. All those with it and all those without it, all listening to the marimbas. The hot night air trills with the gurgling bird harps and echoes with the vibrant plummy, plinky, plonky marimbas. You feel as though you are taking part in the first half finale of some extravagant revue. But then you often do in Mexico. Oh it's quite a place, is Veracruz.

It was in Veracruz that we came across this man selling live beetles. I'm sorry, but some days go like this in Mexico. You see some startling things. He was selling these beetles on the street corner. Big beetles, as big as the top joint of your thumb and these beetles were covered in jewels. Not real jewels, of course, imitation emeralds, rubies and diamonds stuck to the beetle's back. And from its big black left hind leg trails a fine gold chain and a tiny clip so that you can anchor him down wherever you please.

'Er, what are these beetles for?'

'For, señor?'

'Yes, *for*. What are they for?'

'To have, to put on to the table.'

'For decoration?'

'Si, for decoration.'

'To wear on a dress?'

'To wear on a dress, if you like, si.' The beetle crawls up the side of a small box to demonstrate that it could hang on to the flattest bosom with ease if necessary, its jewels flashing in the sun.

'But how long does it live?'

'It will live for about one year.'

'A year?'

'Si, señor.'

'But you've got to give it something to eat—what does it live on?'

'It eats wood, señor.'

'Wood?'

'Si señor, wood. An especial wood, with each beetle I will give you enough wood to last it for the whole year. You like one, señor?'

'No, thanks.'

'Why, señor, it is very beautiful.'

'No, I just don't like the idea of a beetle chained up with jewels on.'

'But señor, be reasonable, be reasonable. I have seen pictures in the magazines of your ladies in the big cities with these poodles, these poodle dogs and these poodle dogs are

wearing jewels around the necks, jewels around the necks I
have seen and they are always on the chains, always on the
chains, that's very bad because the poodles like to run. These
beetles don't like to run, they like to stay still and these
poodles like to bark, the beetles don't make a noise always
very quiet you can sleep the whole day and the poodles is
eating all the time, very expensive things is eating, and the
beetles is eating only a little bit of wood, just a little bit of
wood. The poodles is costing to buy 100, 200, 600 dollars, the
beautiful beetles is costing, not one dollar, just seventy-five
cents. That's reasonable, señor, hey that's reasonable.'

'Yes, that's reasonable.'

'You like?'

'Er. No thanks.'

'Okay señor, okay.'

He's not a bit put out, he smiles, some day you like to buy
one, perhaps. And the dazzling jewelled beetle lumbers
around at the end of his golden tether, crowned with a
glittering diadem like a king emperor and eating wood for
dinner.

'You know, for a moment I thought you were going to buy
one of those beetles.'

'Oh be reasonable Tubby, be reasonable.'

'That's the point, he sounded so reasonable, the beetle
seller.'

I know. That's the trouble—anything that happens here,
no matter what, you must regard in a reasonable light
because there is a very good reason for it. I mean, take that
restaurant where we had breakfast several times this week. It
was a thoroughly nice restaurant. Clean, tidy, charming
waiters over-anxious to serve and to please, spotlessly clean
and immaculately dressed. And yet, swabbing about
amongst the tables the whole time we are having our
breakfast is the biggest thug you ever saw in your life. We call
him Bertie. He has an enormous body the size and shape of a
36-gallon beer barrel with a square shaved wooden head
nailed to the top of it. It looks as though it's nailed on
because his whole hulk moves in one ponderous piece. And
he mops away at the flood with his great squelch mop and

bucket of muddy water and all he wears is a dirty grey vest and a pair of old trousers that hitch underneath his great stomach like a tight chinstrap. It is a vulgar sight, to be sure. Not only that, but he's rather an envious dissatisfied character and as he swabs around our table he watches our plates to see what we are eating. He's never had a breakfast like that, how can we sit there and eat breakfast while the likes of him have to swab floors?

'Come on, Tubby, you'd better finish up all your toast or Bertie will thump you.'

It's strange to have all these pleasant smartly dressed waiters bring your bacon and egg and this half-naked monster Bertie glowering around as you eat. Still, somebody's got to swab up, be reasonable.

He's there every morning and yesterday morning I thought he would thump us. We had a bit of trouble yesterday. A peculiar bit of trouble. There was pepper in the milk, yes, pepper in the milk. Well, it was either pepper or tobacco or one of the explosive firework flavourings. It's a shock when you start to eat up your cornflakes like a good boy, nicely sugared, plenty of wholesome body-building milk, when suddenly after a seven-second delayed action the old snap, crackle, pop, bangs in your head. Your ears buzz, your eyes water.

'Oh gosh, wow, they've let the fireworks loose into something.'

'Must be in the milk, the coffee tastes like curry!'

Well it was all put right quite quickly, the waiters came running—very sorry, dear dear very bad, very bad something has happened please very sorry—but all the time the commotion was on Bertie stood right by our table scowling at us. We had better watch it, that's all. We had better be reasonable, any show of irritation, any sign of temper and he'd thump somebody, so watch it. Oh yes, we are fairly wary of Bertie. But he's not so bad really.

Well, just consider what's happening now. He has just swabbed the entire restaurant and it's shining bright and now the dustmen have arrived. English dustmen are pretty colourful characters as a rule, so are Mexican dustmen, only more so and their dust is more so too. The dustmen, two of them, come strolling through the restaurant, passing the time of day with the smart waiters. They only want the dustbins, that's all. Well the dustbins are in the kitchens and there's no back entrance. They've got to come out this way. And come out this way they do. Rich ripe dustbins overflowing with kitchen swill—don't look at them, don't think about them, get on with your scrambled egg, be reasonable, be reasonable, you can't have all that muck piling up in the kitchen, be reasonable. Bertie is being very reasonable, he knows it can't be helped, the dustmen have to come in and out this way and he's mopping up behind them, he mops up behind everyone. He mops up behind that tall striding Indian woman who comes lunging through the restaurant on her way to the kitchens with a hundredweight of onions perched on her head; he mops up behind the little shrivelled creature who scurries through with a couple of live chickens. Be reasonable, restaurants need these things to cook and they'll buy things from those that bring them, and if the only way to the kitchens is through the dining room, well, you must be reasonable. Bertie, we decide in the end, is more than reasonable.

And the longer we stay in Mexico, I'm pleased to say, the more reasonable we become. After all the people do try. They try like anything to please, and give you what you want.

The trouble of course, is the aeroplane. The aeroplane has upset everything. Well, it's brought all these strange people into the country. People who would never have been able to get there if it hadn't been for the aeroplane. And now the aeroplanes are suddenly flying all over Mexico. Flying to towns that have never had visitors before, or only a few perhaps, bringing in people with strange habits, peculiar tastes, funny whims and fancies. You can't find out about all these funny people in five minutes you know. It takes time. Mexico isn't quite ready yet, catching up mind you, and it's learning as fast as it can, but it's not quite ready yet in places and so you must be reasonable.

And you should be reasonable if you consider that we

expect these people to change overnight just to suit us. Oh no, it does no harm to be reasonable, although it's a bit of a strain at times.

CHAPTER SEVENTEEN

The Laughter of the Thais

Now I have knocked about a bit in the last few years. And a knock about life knocks a lot of nonsense out of you and fortunately knocks a bit of sense into you. You learn a lot of the wicked ways of this world—of the evil wiles of men and women and advertising agents. I have known for years that most picture posters depicting the attractions of any country you like to mention are false. Frauds.

All those lovely girls in national costume. Do you ever see them? Of course you don't. All those handsome men belting about on horses by the seashore. Does it ever happen to you? No. Dining by candlelight with all those smashers soaking champagne? Out of the question. Fishing in a gurgling river with a 25 lb salmon on the end of your line? Huh, don't be funny. You can't tell me.

Oh, but you can. You see, I *believed* Bangkok. I believed every poster I saw of Bangkok. I don't know why, but I did. I thought they were true, fool that I was and they're not. Bangkok is not what the posters say it is.

I don't think I have ever been so shocked and disappointed by any city anywhere. There are bright and lovely jewels of buildings to be found in Bangkok, but they are all but choked to death—drowned in a tidal wave of concrete. Bangkok is now an enormous city. It's like the enormous cities of the American Middle West. It has the overall ugliness of cheap, thoughtless slap-happy building. Building for business. Doesn't matter what it looks like, doesn't matter what you pull down, there's money to be made in that dead, square concrete. There's gold in them there concrete boxes, pure gold.

And they are building them by the million in Bangkok, plastering them with money-spinning neon signs, flashing the messages of coke and cars, bowling alleys, motels and cinemas. Raising the standard of living, they say. What standard? Just look at the street we are sitting in now. Sitting in a taxi in a sweltering traffic jam. The traffic is impossible. You might be in any of those American cities where, judging by the evidence of your eyes, the general IQ of the population is somewhere in the neighbourhood of $1\frac{1}{4}$.

'How long have we been sitting in this cab?'

'Oh, getting on for ten minutes. I suppose we'll move in a minute.'

The driver turns on his radio: 'You are tuned in to the American Forces Network and the (ding-dong) time is eleven o'clock, the temperature is 88 degrees and once again we bring you the news every hour on the hour.' The driver clicks the radio off. He doesn't want to hear the news, neither do we.

'The ding-dong time is eleven o'clock, so they say.'

'Yes. I prefer the tick-tock time myself,' Tubby says.

'Well if we don't move soon we'll still be sitting here when the next tick-tock, ding-dong news time comes around.'

'I think we are moving.'

'So we are.'

We creep and crawl with the millions of other cars and taxis that honk and roar in the cheap and nasty streets of this hot and dusty city. Bangkok is a terrible disappointment to begin with. That's the point, you see. The longer you stay the better it becomes. The concrete and the traffic and the heat become just an irritation, a nuisance preventing you from seeing what is left of what must have been a little dream city. The city that the posters say it is.

And bit by bit you find it. The palaces, the temples hiding behind the concrete and the one or two that are left to stand and breathe freely and tinkle their windbells in the breeze. There's the temple of the Emerald Buddha. It's the sort of place you really can't believe.

I often wonder if what I saw at the temple of the Emerald

Buddha was really true. I remember standing looking at it and chuckling with sheer happiness. Oh, the brilliant, clever, pretty people who built it. Happy people who can build to make you chortle with glee. The children and the fairies built it. They built it with magic and multi-coloured glass, millions and millions of tiny squares of coloured glass. A tremendous mosaic of shattering colour, sparkling and winking back at the sun. Golden domes, mottled dragons, fearful giants, golden cockerels. The whole place shimmers like a fantastic mirage and a fitful breeze tickles the windbells that flutter in the eaves. It is the most hilarious, ingenious, architectural giggle. A chortle of gaiety and brilliance, a ripple of utter delight. The children built it with their laughter. The dear pretty little children. They built it as they played so innocently, so prettily and with such devoted love. They made a building to make you smile with joy and glow with a profound pleasure, and when you turn to leave this happiness a painful lump swells in your throat because you know all the children are dead. Dead and gone. Only the ogres are left. Ogres with concrete slopping from their chops.

It must be painful for the people who live in Bangkok to see their city change so quickly. To watch the ugliness spread over so much that was so pretty. And the Thai people are very pretty people. They are if anything even smaller than the Malays. Beautifully made, little hand-carved ornaments. I am by no means a tall person yet I feel like a sawn-off giant amongst all these little pretties.

Well, take the three that live at the end of the corridor. Three children live at the end of the corridor in our hotel. They are employed by the hotel and wear hotel uniform. There's one little girl who wears a uniform sarong and two little boys who wear sort of bell-boy outfits. Their job is to answer the service bell, tidy your room, see that the vacuum flask is full of iced water. I suppose they are about fourteen or fifteen years old but they look no more than eleven. They are beautiful children. Perfect little faces, immaculate white teeth. You can't help noticing their teeth because they are always gurgling with laughter. They are at an age when you are liable to get that terrible laughter paralysis, when your whole diaphragm seizes up and bends you over in an awful grip. When you believe you are dying in ecstasy. And there's nothing you can do about it. But that's not all. The moment you get over one attack of paralysis you may have another one, any second. Someone only has to say a few funny words like wobbly blancmange and off you go again. In exquisite agony.

The three little ones at the end of the corridor suffer in this way. Whenever we ring the bell for, say, some iced water, the three of them come giggling into the room. One of them could do it easily but they're friends you see and so they all come.

'Can we have some iced water please?'

'*Heheheheheh*, oh dear iced water, *hahahah*, iced water, *heheheheh*, iced water.'

You have no *idea* how funny iced water is—*hahahaha*. One takes the vacuum flask, another the glasses, another the tray and they go to get the funny iced water. They are back in a couple of minutes, *heheheheh*, oh dear this iced water is killing them, *hehehehehe*.

One day they brought the iced water when I was shaving with a cordless electric razor. They stopped their sniggering the moment they heard it and came over and stared at me. Three faces hardly a foot away staring with concentrated curiosity. Like three intense medical students watching a complicated surgical operation for the first time. Occasionally a little hand just touches my face after the razor has rasped around, just to try. And they are simply astonished at the grotesque shaving faces I pull when I mow around the edges and into the corners.

When I have finished the operation they ask if they might try. I hand the razor to one of the boys. He puts it to his chin and switches it on, *brbrbrbrb*. Oh dear, that tickles him to death, he is stricken with the laughing paralysis. The others try and they too succumb.

But they will soon snap out of it and pay attention if you speak firmly. One evening they came giggling into the room with the funny iced water. We take whisky and iced water every evening about seven o'clock, but this evening . . . 'I don't know, Tubby, would you like a beer instead?'

'Yes, very nice. Yes a small bottle of beer would be very nice.'

'Yes, well you know, I think I could drink a big bottle of beer.'

So we want one big bottle and one small bottle. The kids ought to be able to manage that, but we have never asked them to get this before so I'll have to be loud and clear to make them understand.

'Look, do you think you could get for us one big bottle of beer and one small bottle of beer?' They listen carefully and very conscientiously. I say it again. 'One big bottle of beer and one small bottle of beer.'

One lad has got it. He repeats, 'One big boc, one small boc.'

'That's it one big bottle and one small bottle.'

'One big boc, one small boc.'

Well, that gives them something different to do and they scuttle away. Half an hour later we are still waiting for them to come back.

'What do you think has happened to them?'

'No idea, they've only to go down to the ground floor and back.'

'Do you think they've forgotten?'

'They never forget a thing.'

It was then we heard the rumpus in the corridor, a noise of someone moving a wardrobe or a washing machine or waltzing with a double bass. Our door opens and the kids come struggling, giggling in, pushing and pulling some great packing case. They drag it to the middle of the room. There we are, how about that, didn't think we could do it, did you? They are terribly pleased with themselves. In the middle of the room stands an enormous cardboard box. The sort of box that would hold a refrigerator. They open the lid and take out of the big box one small box. There we are, that's what you wanted, wasn't it? One big box and one small box, you said it three times, one big box one small box. There you are, took a bit of doing I can tell you—in just over a half an hour one big box, one small box.

'Oh dear, what can we tell them?'

'I don't know, it'll break their little hearts.'

'Yes, they've probably been all over Bangkok for those boxes.'

They stand there smiling and yet their brown eyes are perplexed and hurt because we haven't shown the slightest sign of gratitude and it's clear that one big box and one small box is not what we want at all. It's terrible.

'Look, that's very nice, thank you very much, but you see we really wanted a big bottle.'

It takes a long time to explain to them the subtle difference between a big bottle and a big box and a small bottle and a small box. But when the message gets through, oh dear, a slow laughing paralysis seizes them all. They collapse on the floor around the cardboard boxes and it's another half an hour before they are able to think about getting the big bottle of beer and the small bottle of beer. And now, whenever we meet them on the stairs or in the corridor, we have only to mumble those excruciatingly funny, magic words, 'Big bottle' and they die laughing slowly on the spot.

I suppose they are under some sort of supervision in this hotel but it's not very apparent. Well, you can't be watching them for twelve to fifteen hours a day. That's the time they are on duty, so it seems. So is everyone else in the hotel. The girls in the coffee shop, the girls in reception, the girls who serve in the arcade shops, they never seem to go home—if they have homes—they are always there. Always dignified, always beautifully groomed, always charming. They are such self-contained little creatures. They have the measure of everything, and you feel that they could cope with an earthquake.

The girl in the bookshop, for instance: I went in there one evening at about eleven o'clock to buy a postcard or two. Well, the lights were still on but there was nobody about. *Mmm*, I cross to the postcard stand and give it a spin and then I see her, sound asleep behind the counter. The noise of the postcard stand turning gets through to her. She doesn't wake up with a fluster or a skirmish. Somehow she miraculously becomes alive and in one graceful movement levitates herself and lands beside the postcard stand, composed and smiling. It's uncanny. I can't apologise for waking her because I can't believe that two seconds ago she was asleep. She would hate me to apologise or to even suggest that I had caught her nodding off.

I choose a couple of postcards. Better let people know how we are getting on, where we are going to be. That's just it—we don't know. Our visas for Burma have not come through yet. Tomorrow we had better call once again at the British Embassy to see if they've turned up.

A tremendous bronze statue of Queen Victoria sits in the grounds of the British Embassy in Bangkok. The old lady is seated on a throne in full regalia and she must weigh every bit of 200 tons. Day after day she sits in the middle of the lawn in the blazing sun and sweats. Yes, the statue sweats. Perhaps it's condensation or an accidental flick of the gardener's hose, but there the old queen sits and sweats. But even so, though she's cast in hundreds of tons of bronze, you feel like dropping a curtsey to her as you pass.

Everyone is frightfully nice at the embassy. They can't think what's happened to the visas: 'It's not this end, you understand, it's the Burmese in Rangoon. Visas should be here. Try again tomorrow or, look here, I tell you what, take the bull by the horns and go around to the Burmese Embassy.'

All right, tomorrow we'll try the Burmese Embassy. Well there is no point in both of us going, one of us should do it, leaving the other one time for a spot of shopping. And we toss for it and Tubby is chosen to go alone to the Burmese Embassy . . .

Now the Burmese Embassy is in a very pleasant, residential part of Bangkok. And so are many other embassies. Embassies tend to group together. And on this fine and cheerful morning Tubby Foster, our diplomat of the year, began his negotiations to obtain visas for us to enter Burma. A very pleasant gentleman in a neat suit approaches him as he enters the reception hall. He is one of the normal-channel chaps.

'Good morning sir, what can I do for you this morning?'

'Oh good morning, lovely one isn't it, well I've come about the visas.'

'Oh yes sir, what visas?'

'Here we are.'

I will say this for Tubby—he puts on a very good diplomatic show. He always carries on these occasions a very convincing diplomatic briefcase crammed full with papers, pamphlets, folders, notebooks, dictionaries, pens, pencils, cigarettes and a few packets of fruit drops. Cigarettes and fruit drops are very useful in any diplomatic negotiations. They are way-pavers, says Tubby, they pave the way. If the normal-channel chap doesn't smoke, ten to one he'll go for a fruit drop.

But this morning this normal-channel chap rejects Tubby's way-pavers. He's been told never to accept sweets from strange men. So Tubby gets straight on with the business. He brings out a fistful of papers.

'Here we are then, visas required for Morris and Foster.'

'Yes sir. Why do you want visas?'

Ah now, careful, the normal-channel chap is putting out a rather unnormal feeler. 'Why do we want visas? Well you know, to have a look around and that, no harm meant, you understand, it's all on the forms.'

'Oh yes sir, but why do you ask for visas?'

He's a deep one, this one is. 'Well you see, we thought it would be rather nice.'

'Sir, you do not need visas to enter my country.'

'What did you say?'

'You do not need visas to enter my country.'

'No visas?'

'No sir.'

It was then that Tubby became thoroughly undiplomatic. He said: 'Don't talk blinking daft, don't talk so blinking, flipping daft. Of course you need visas, we've filled up about fifty forms, had our photographs taken twice a day, of course we need visas—what the hell are you playing at? What the hell are you playing at?'

The normal-channel chap winces. 'Sir, excuse me, but

215

what country do you wish to go to?'

'Well, Burma of course, Burma.'

'But sir, this is the Indian Embassy.'

'The Indian Embassy?'

'Yes sir.'

At that point the talks—as they say—broke down. Tubby blames the taxi driver. Well, the Indian Embassy and the Burmese Embassy are next door to one another and the taxi driver dropped Tubby in between the two. Nevertheless it's a pretty severe diplomatic defeat, Tubby. 'Oh yes, I know.' It's going to look ghastly on your annual report to the Foreign Secretary: tried to open negotiations at wrong embassy. I wonder if it's ever happened before? I wouldn't be surprised if a lot of our diplomatic missions are carried out in the wrong embassies judging by the outcome, but at least you did find out you were in the wrong embassy. Some of them never do. Yes, very embarrassing.

And no luck next door at the right embassy? 'No, not a sausage. Everything still going through the normal channels.'

But the normal channels are long and devious, the normal channels are clogged with silt. We go every day and ask how the normal channels are getting on. And the answer is always the same. They are normal—which means that nothing happens. As they say, nobody don't know nuffink. And so we decide to do the next best thing. If we are not to be allowed into Burma, we'll go and have a look at it. Even if it's only a distant Burmese mountain. And so we do. We take an aeroplane from Bangkok to the northern town of Chiangami in Thailand.

We hired a car and a driver and went up into the hills. Well, we just wanted to look across at Burma far away in the distance and we hoped we might be able to come across some of the hill tribes who live around here. Whether or not we saw Burma I cannot say. We climbed a high wooded mountain and looked in the direction of Burma. It's just a chain of mountains standing in staggered formation one behind the other.

'Well, I think that the fifteenth mountain back is probably

Burma, don't you?'

'Yes I should say so, looks very nice doesn't it?'

It was when we were coming down the mountain that we met one of the hill tribesmen, a wiry little chap dressed in black, with a squinney little face, a silver bangle around his neck and a red bandeau around his forehead. He carries a crossbow and a quiver of arrows. He knows our driver and he's obviously quite used to tourists because he comes straight over to us and immediately offers me a toffee. Yes, a toffee. Well, that's what I thought it was. And it's not exactly a gift, it's strictly a cash transaction. He wants money for it.

Of course it wasn't toffee, our driver knew what it was at once. Neatly wrapped in greaseproof paper, you open it and this soft, half-melted toffee is opium. Yes, opium. It is of course illegal to trade in opium. But what can you do? The chaps around here have always done it. It stands to reason—you get as much money by growing a few square yards of poppies as you do by growing a couple of acres of rice.

And it's so easy to market, make it up into toffees and stick them inside your shirt. No, it's not all that risky. Of course there are nosey parkers about, but they've got a job to find a tiny patch of poppies growing in all the thousands of miles of rolling mountains up here.

Well, what about it? Do I want the opium, a couple of bob, there you are? Not really, I wouldn't know what to do with it.

'Wouldn't know what to do with it? Come on, this way.' We follow our little squinney friend up a wooded track and he leads us to his village.

The village is beautifully situated on the side of a hill, little thatched huts just strewn about any old how. The only sign of order is the water system. The water comes from a mountain stream and it's conducted to various points in the village along large bamboo poles. It's very simple, the bamboo poles are just sliced in half to make a sort of guttering, the guttering is propped up on forked sticks and there you have a bamboo aqueduct with constant fresh mountain water at your door. What more do you want? The hill tribes certainly seem to need very little. They do like their silver bangles around their little necks though. Nearly all wear them. Men, women and children with silver bangles around their necks, bandeaus around their little heads and black trousers and shirts.

What's going on over there? A dozen little boys are playing tops. They are playing with such energy and with such concentration. It's the same game of tops that we used to play. One side spin their tops in the middle and the other side send their tops spinning amongst them trying to knock them over.

'We used to play this game,' said Tubby.

'I know. They are a bit behind the times here, aren't they?'

'Look, we've got to go in there.'

Oh, our squinney friend is calling us into a hut. We go in. It's dark and smoky. Dark because there are no windows, and smoky because there's a wood fire and no chimney. One or two dark human forms are lying around. In the middle of the floor burns a small lamp. It burns with the yellow flame of animal fat. Beside the fat yellow flame lies a man. His flickering face is close to the lamp, a face so drawn, so ill, so near death. He looks to be embalmed—his skin is the shade of a tallow candle. He's smoking opium. Lying beside the puny fluttering flame lies this withering mummy. A few more puffs and he will surely disappear before our very eyes. Our squinney friend asks our driver if we would like a go.

'Well no, not for me thanks, what about you?'

'No, I don't think so. I was always told smoking was bad for you, now I'm sure it is.'

'Yes, wonder how long he'll last?'

Wonder how long it will all last, the peace and tranquillity of Chiangmai.

There's a little village a few miles from Chiangmai where they make sunshades. The whole village makes sunshades—it has done so for years. Paper sunshades. Pretty paper sunshades and they make them at home. It's a cottage industry and the cottages have little courtyards, and the courtyards are littered with sunshades—sunshades fully open in the midday sun, fresh-painted sunshades drying in the sun. In the courtyards, in the streets, in the gardens lie the charming little tasselled sunshades.

Each family its own little factory. They make their own paper from the pounded and pulped bark of a tree, a lovely fibrous, hand-made paper. They sit in their gardens in the shade and paste the paper to the bony sunshade frames, layer after layer of paper. After each layer comes a smalming of lacquer.

The girls are pasting, pasting, holding the stems of the sunshades in their toes. The daughters of the households are spinning and pasting, trimming and turning sunshades in their toes.

'Just look at this little pet!'

'How old is she, nine or ten?' She's obviously the cleverest little minx in the family because she's doing the most important bit, painting on the flower and bird decorations. Sprays of flowers, fluttering birds. All done free-hand. She uses a small, rather flat brush. One half of the bristles she dips in white paint, the other half in the red so she can paint with two colours at the same time. The brush in her little hand scampers about with all the childish gaiety of the nine-year-old brain that controls it. Posies of flowers just grow and blossom, little birds fly in and hover. She is a little genius.

Tararara!

'Where's that music coming from?' I ask.

'Somewhere over there, I think.'

We wander off towards the music, across a tiny field full of sunshades drying. In the next field they are cutting the rice. A dozen boys and girls and their parents are cutting the rice by hand, laying it out in sheaves. *Taararararararar.* It's quite uncanny, the music is coming from nowhere. The golden rice fields stretch away to the mountains, the lazy white clouds just hang about in the blue—*tararararar.*

'This is weird, isn't it?'

'Yes, most peculiar. It seems to be coming more from that direction.'

We walk through the sheaves of rice. *Tarararar.* It's almost on top of us, *tarara.* Huh, there it is! Hidden under a couple of sheaves of rice is a rather smart radio—*tarararar.*

'Mmm. That's it then, radio in the rice fields, music while you work.'

'Yes, things are catching up with them, aren't they?'

'Yes. I wonder how long it'll be before the terrible pace of our civilisation gets through and swamps them.'

'Oh, take a long time yet.'

'Mmm, maybe you're right. If our civilisation has to get here through the normal channels, well you know what the normal channels are . . . it will take a time, thank goodness, a *heck* of a time.'

'Yes, a heck of a time,' agreed Tubby.